D1644126

PRAISE FOR
Under the Cover of Light

"[Col. Curtis's] staunch resistance in the face of grueling physical and emotional treatment made him an outstanding example of what it means to stay committed to faith and country, no matter the cost."

COL JOE KITTINGER, USAF (RET.)

UNDER THE COVER OF LIGHT

The Extraordinary Story of
USAF COL Thomas "Jerry" Curtis's
7½-Year Captivity in North Vietnam

CAROLE ENGLE AVRIETT

TYNDALE
MOMENTUM™

The nonfiction imprint of
Tyndale House Publishers, Inc.

Visit Tyndale online at www.tyndale.com.

Visit Tyndale Momentum online at www.tyndalemomentum.com.

TYNDALE, *Tyndale Momentum*, and Tyndale's quill logo are registered trademarks of Tyndale House Publishers, Inc. The Tyndale Momentum logo is a trademark of Tyndale House Publishers, Inc. Tyndale Momentum is the nonfiction imprint of Tyndale House Publishers, Inc., Carol Stream, Illinois.

Under the Cover of Light: The Extraordinary Story of USAF COL Thomas "Jerry" Curtis's 7½-Year Captivity in North Vietnam

Copyright © 2017 by Carole Engle Avriett. All rights reserved.

Cover photograph of cement copyright © pashabo/Depositphotos. All rights reserved.

Illustrations copyright © 2017 by Bret A. Melvin/www.bucktoothstudios.com. All rights reserved.

Author photograph of Carole Avriett by Sarah Sandel Photography, copyright © 2016. All rights reserved.

Designed by Eva Winters

Edited by Jonathan Schindler

Published in association with the literary agency of WordServe Literary Group, www.wordserveliterary.com.

Unless otherwise indicated, all Scripture quotations are taken from the *Holy Bible*, King James Version.

Scripture quotations marked ESV are taken from *The Holy Bible*, English Standard Version® (ESV®), copyright © 2001 by Crossway, a publishing ministry of Good News Publishers. Used by permission. All rights reserved.

ISBN 978-1-4964-2156-2   Hardcover
ISBN 978-1-4964-2157-9   Softcover

Printed in the United States of America

23   22   21   20   19   18   17
7   6   5   4   3   2   1

To Terry:
Faithful before, faithful during, faithful now . . .
Faithful with enduring love.

—Jerry

No one ever expects to encounter truly devastating circumstances in their lives. I know I didn't. But if you have a relationship with God, he helps you meet those challenges with hope. Confidence in him is never misplaced. He has remained with me through the years—without him, I could not have done the things I've been called upon to do.

COLONEL THOMAS "JERRY" CURTIS, USAF (RET.),

POW 1965–1973

In him was life, and the life was the light of men. The light shines in the darkness, and the darkness has not overcome it.

JOHN 1:4–5, ESV

CONTENTS

FOREWORD

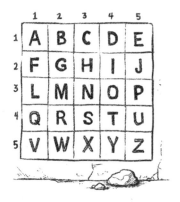

	1	2	3	4	5
1	A	B	C	D	E
2	F	G	H	I	J
3	L	M	N	O	P
4	Q	R	S	T	U
5	V	W	X	Y	Z

CAPTAIN TOM CURTIS was the pilot of an HH-43 helicopter that was shot down in September 1965 in North Vietnam during an attempt to rescue an Air Force pilot whose F-105 fighter bomber had previously been shot down by heavy ground fire.

For men in combat who are in need of help or may later be in a position to require assistance, men involved in SAR (Search and Rescue) are *all* heroes. These SAR men disregard their own safety to help save the lives of downed comrades in arms. And most of the time they fly into zones where there is heavy resistance from an enemy who has already inflicted losses on our forces. Nevertheless, they search for, find, and rescue the wounded soldiers or downed airmen—often at great peril to themselves.

That was exactly what happened to Tom Curtis and his crew of four when he tried to extract a downed F-105 fighter pilot.

All but one of Tom's crew were captured by North Vietnamese soldiers. Tom's copilot evaded capture for a short time but was captured by the Pathet Lao in nearby Laos. He later was killed in an escape attempt.

My F-105 fighter was shot down about five months earlier than Tom and his other crewmen. I was captured immediately when my parachute touched me down near the bridge (at Thanh Hoa), which I had just bombed. My captors were very angry. After two days of gross mistreatment they trucked me to a large prison in Hanoi, which we called the Hanoi Hilton—where torture, interrogation, and solitary confinement continued. Any communication with other POWs was forbidden. After a month or two I was pulled from my cell and taken to another, larger cell to join three other American POWs. In a couple of days one other POW joined us. We were all overjoyed to be together.

At an Air Force Survival School (before leaving the States) I heard an instructor tell about POWs in a German camp in World War II communicating between buildings by tapping on a common water pipe. As I left class, I found the instructor walking by me, so I asked him how they sent the dashes—thinking it was the Morse code. He quickly took me to the chalkboard and showed me the "tap code" they used.

It was a five-by-five matrix of the alphabet, omitting *K*. We used *C* for *K*. The first line was *ABCDE*, and the first column was *AFLQV*. To use the code, one would first tap one to five times to identify the *A*, *F*, *L*, *Q*, or *V* row, pause, and tap one to five times to identify the letter in that row. Thus the letter *S* would be tapped *AFLQ*, pause, *QRS*. I taught this code to the others in the large cell. Within a few days our captors put us all back in solitary confinement, and we successfully tapped to our comrades in adjacent cells. Recognizing the importance of communicating, we went to great lengths to ensure that every POW knew the tap code. It spread like a chain reaction.

The importance of communication between POWs cannot be overstated. It was a morale booster. It provided a vehicle for the POW chain of command to be utilized. It provided for shared information to counter the efforts of the enemy to divide the POWs and for POWs, under the direction of the senior ranking officer (SRO), to form a common resistance to their aims. It provided information from friends and family back home (from later shoot-downs). It provided educational opportunities from a wealth of knowledge (all POWs shared a need to make some productive use of time spent in prison). Communicating, clearing for guards, and all efforts to assist the communication process (not limited to just the tap code) used a great amount of time each day.

Through the tap code, POWs gained the strength of unity. Shared information of torture and mistreatment created a peer pressure for every POW to resist to the best of his ability and group support for those who were already resisting. Our captors tortured us to obtain propaganda statements. With the richness of our language we used double meanings, slang, lies, and other means to make those statements unusable. We developed great pride in ourselves and in our fellow POWs through our resistance. We, under difficult circumstances, operated as an effective organization to counter our captors' efforts to exploit us. Communication helped us to come home with honor, knowing that in the end we prevailed over a brutal enemy. We won our war!

Through our covert communication in the Hanoi Hilton, I learned of Tom's incarceration. Later, in November 1970, the POW camp at Son Tay was attacked by our armed forces to free American POWs. Unfortunately, all POWs had been moved from that camp by the North Vietnamese a short time earlier. Within three days our captors closed all the small POW camps (fearing another raid) and trucked us back to the Hanoi Hilton.

By now we could not be put back in small cells—there were too many of us (about 360). So our captors put us in large cells with up to forty men to a cell. That was great for us. And that is where I got to know Tom Curtis very well. Tom, I, and others worked together to successfully put coded messages in the six-line letters our captors occasionally permitted us to write home. Tom was one of the most respected POWs in our cell—a tough resister, a leader, responsible, industrious, and a true friend.

One final thought. We endured a lot, including time away from family and an inability to have a normal life with all the freedoms this country provides. Nevertheless, I believe that in retrospect, most (if not all) returned POWs recognize now that the net effect of our incarceration is a positive in our lives. Those bad times no longer haunt us. While there, we had time to better form and strengthen our values. We learned the value of prayer. While we didn't immediately obtain the miracles we prayed for, we received greater gifts of much more value—patience, knowledge that we were not alone, the will to go on, a sense of worth, and an optimistic view of the future with a greater closeness to our God. Those miracles that we prayed for all occurred and more—just not on our time schedule but on God's.

I cherish the brotherhood I experience even now with the many returned POWs, especially with men like Tom Curtis, who came home with honor. I am honored to be able to write this foreword.

CARLYLE "SMITTY" HARRIS
COLONEL, USAF, RETIRED

AUTHOR'S NOTE

FEW MILITARY HISTORY accounts are more inspiring than those produced by the prisoner-of-war experience in Southeast Asia in the sixties and seventies. Men of faith and commitment to family and country displayed what it meant to endure debilitating hardships yet emerge with honor and dignity.

This is the story of one of those POWs, Thomas "Jerry" Curtis, a brave man yet full of grace, who began trusting God as a young boy and maintained trust even through 2,703 days of captivity in the prison system of Hanoi, Vietnam.

What Jerry learned in captivity about the Light of mankind has never been more relevant than it is today, for we live in times that are increasingly dark and challenging with powerful forces of both good and evil looming on the horizon. His story is a message of triumph over adversity, of courage and hope, commitment and endurance. Above all else, it is a testimony that even in the blackest night, Light remains in the world—it cannot be conquered, and it will not fail.

PROLOGUE

ONE MORNING in late April 1966, in Houston, Texas, Dr. Michael Ellis DeBakey discovered that his patient's heart had stopped during a valve-replacement procedure. The physician was the first to use a mechanical heart pump in a human, saving the patient's life and ushering in all future open-heart surgeries. At the same time, on the other side of the world and in drastically different circumstances, another Houston son experienced his own heart-stopping moment.

A sudden grinding of the lock on his cell door in Briarpatch, the most primitive camp within Hanoi's prison system, caused Captain Thomas "Jerry" Curtis to sit bolt upright. It was too late in the morning for turnkeys to bring his plate of worm-filled rice with boiled pumpkin and too early in the day for his bowl of thin cabbage stock. An unscheduled visit could mean only one of three things: a session of prolonged physical abuse, intensive interrogation laced with propaganda, or both.

Since his shoot-down seven months earlier on September 20, 1965, the rescue-helicopter pilot already had endured sadistic guards all too eager to administer punishment. The possibility of what might lie ahead on that April morning filled him with incredible anxiety. Adrenaline surged. His heart pounded.

As the door banged open, an armed guard rushed into the small cell. He motioned at the prisoner with a chopping movement to the wrists, a sign for Jerry to put on his long-sleeved shirt, part of his striped prison uniform. Pulling the coarse cotton tunic over his head suddenly seemed a monumental task. He left the shirt hanging out, a required sign of subservience.

Jerry labored to stay focused as he was shoved down a narrow corridor to another solid masonry room where the camp commander waited. Nicknamed "Frenchy" by POWs because he spoke English with a heavy French accent, the North Vietnamese officer seemed not to notice the captive's entrance. The guard motioned for Jerry to sit on the low, child-sized stool directly in front of a large wooden desk behind which Frenchy wielded authority.

From his elevated position, Frenchy began, slowly and methodically, outlining his prisoner's dilemma. His quiet rant explored all the ways Jerry no longer had anyone or anything he could rely on.

"You are . . . blackest of criminals. You . . . no longer have military, no government, no country." He drew each word out, savoring his control over his prisoner. "You . . . no longer have family for support. If you get sick, no doctor will come unless

I say. You have no friends who can help you. You do not have possessions or job or resources, whatsoever. You . . . have no food . . . not even sip of water unless I say so. You are completely alone . . . and vulnerable."

After what seemed an eternity, the North Vietnamese officer, obviously pleased with his monologue, delivered its summation, a final statement intended to underscore the prisoner's hellish situation. "Now, here in this place, you have only me to rely on . . ." The commander's voice trailed off, and then he added, ". . . and your God."

Frenchy meant that last comment to further debilitate the man hunched on the stool before him. Surely such a man, captured, beaten, and with little hope of escape, must have been abandoned by God. But Frenchy's words had just the opposite effect. They spoke directly to Jerry's inner strength. He felt a surge of hope, a penetrating ray of extreme light in a moment of utter darkness.

In the years following his release from Hanoi, Jerry often thought back to this moment. Scripture records God frequently using pagan rulers and authorities to do his bidding, sometimes even to say what he wanted said. Pharaoh found himself bending to the Lord's desire to release the Israelites from bondage. Powerful kings—Nebuchadnezzar, Darius, and Artaxerxes—fulfilled with words from their own mouths God's ultimate purposes.

On that particular day, a smug North Vietnamese camp commander representing an atheistic Communist regime and believing himself to be in complete control inadvertently delivered a personal message of hope. Using an unlikely mouthpiece, God planted in the heart of one of his children a definitive reminder of his abiding presence.

PART 1

THE MISSION: COMBAT SEARCH AND RESCUE

CHAPTER 1
THE DINNER PARTY
MAY 24, 1973

SOME SAID ENTERTAINER Sammy Davis Jr. was the first to float the idea for a large soiree honoring returned prisoners of war from Vietnam. Others said First Lady Pat Nixon, during an emotional embrace with Margaret Manhard at a White House reception, had promised a "big celebration" when Mrs. Manhard's husband came home. Philip W. Manhard had been the highest-ranking civilian captured by the Viet Cong and held for five torturous years in the jungles of South Vietnam; both women eagerly awaited his return. Still others thought the idea surfaced in the Oval Office while Cabinet members watched footage of the first freed POWs arriving at Clark Air Force Base aboard a C-141 Starlifter.

Wherever the idea originated, President Richard Milhous

Nixon, amid growing scandal, latched on to it with palpable enthusiasm, and so did the rest of the country. No matter on which side of the war a person's political beliefs landed him or her, nearly everyone thought a party for the POWs was in order.

And who didn't recognize the uniqueness of the occasion? All the returning prisoners—repatriated a short nine weeks earlier and reunited with wives, children, and families, many of whom had not seen one another for as long as eight years—were regarded as heroes. The group quickly attained near-celebrity status. Once the celebration began to take shape, an incredible outpouring of entertainers came forward to participate, some of the best known in show business.

The role of master of ceremonies naturally fell to Bob Hope. John Wayne, Jimmy Stewart, Sammy Davis Jr., Roy Acuff, Joey Heatherton, Vic Damone, Irving Berlin, and Les Brown and His Band of Renown, among others, were eager to perform for the troops gratis. They spent most of the night mingling, shaking hands, and posing for pictures with as many as desired.

Remembering the evening years later, then–presidential military aide Colonel Stephen Bauer said no event in all his six years of working at the White House was "more thrilling, awesome, or satisfying than the celebration held for the just-released prisoners of war." Excitement overflowed to social staff, domestic staff, press corps, guards, police officers. Even the usually stoic Secret Service wore happy smiles and maintained a generally relaxed attitude.

The menu was kept simple, nevertheless hearty: roast sirloin of beef au jus, tiny new potatoes, and selected garden vegetables. A pair of long aluminum canoes filled with ice became unlikely buckets for dozens of bottles of champagne, and two additional Army refrigerator trucks kept hundreds of strawberry mousse desserts and Supreme of Seafood Neptune appetizers with cornsticks chilled at the appropriate thirty-six degrees.

More than thirteen hundred guests attended that evening. The sheer size of the dinner required an enormous tent, longer and wider than the White House itself, covering the south lawn where the president's helicopter normally lands. Underneath the sprawling canvas, hanging chandeliers along with hundreds of votive candles created a serene glow. As guests arrived, dozens of table stewards rushed to put finishing touches on 126 round tables draped with gold cloth, topped by beautiful place settings, flowers, and linens.

It was the largest seated dinner ever given at the White House since John Adams first occupied its still-unfinished interior 215 years ago. It remains so today.

■ ■ ■

In their room at the Statler Hotel, two blocks north of the White House, Lieutenant Colonel Thomas "Jerry" Curtis, in his formal Air Force mess dress uniform with its new silver oak leaves, stood quietly watching his stunning wife clip her pearl earrings into place. The day had been nonstop. That afternoon in the West Auditorium of the Department of State, President Nixon's address to the POWs began with a nearly two-minute standing ovation. The returning POWs as a group would forever think of Nixon as the one who brought them home.

While the honorees listened to their commander in chief, their wives, mothers, and guests were hosted by the first lady and her daughters—Tricia Nixon Cox and Julie Nixon

Eisenhower—in the State Department's formal Diplomatic Reception Rooms. Now the couple was headed to the White House to be honored along with the other POWs at a formal, seated dinner, with entertainment by a host of celebrities, and to meet the president himself: heady events for anyone, much less the youngest of nine children born into a rural Texas subsistence-farming family.

During the 1920s and 1930s, the large Curtis family had farmed acreage near Teague, Texas, outside of Houston. Though they lived "cash poor," especially through the Depression years, what they needed for survival they planted and harvested themselves. Whatever they picked in the garden that day became supper that night. The family was self-reliant, confident, hardworking, and unassuming.

When Emily Parazade Howell Curtis realized she was pregnant with their ninth child, she chose the name "Geraldine," certain she was carrying a girl. During the same time frame, the family leased land from a Mr. Jerry West, who often rode his horse to visit. Between his mother's mistaken intuition and a friendly landowner, the name "Jerry" survived and is what family and close friends call Thomas Curtis today. Air Force friends and acquaintances, however, know him as "Tom," since the military customarily uses first names.

Jerry's father never went to church except for funerals. But his mother led a quiet Christian life, helping neighbors whenever they needed it, displaying a servant's heart as the occasion called for. Very shy as a boy, Jerry dreaded going down to the altar in front of everyone at Cloverleaf Baptist Church. At twelve, however, he felt an irresistible press upon his heart to "walk the aisle" and ask Jesus Christ to be his Savior, even though he had silently done so a year earlier.

After graduating from high school, Jerry commuted back and forth to Houston University's main campus. But a gradual loss of interest in his diesel electric studies plus growing financial need prompted him and some friends to check out the aviation cadet program sponsored by the United States Air Force. Glen Duke, his best friend since sixth grade, went with him.

Jerry had never even been in an airplane. His first flight came as a passenger in a Navion, and Jerry immediately fell in love with flying. He trained with civilian instructors at Kinston, North Carolina, the first twenty hours in the PA-18 Super Cub, then 120 hours in the T-6 Texan. After training in the T-28 and the T-33, Jerry received his wings and a commission as a 2nd Lieutenant on December 18, 1954. For several years afterward, he would fly jets and then transition into helicopters.

Pilot training had required all his attention, to the exclusion of everything else, including faith. So when he finally arrived for his first assignment at Ellington Air Force Base, Houston, several older siblings set out to see he returned to his Christian roots. One of the ways they did this was to invite him to attend a revival service being held at Uvalde Baptist Church, where one of his brothers was a deacon. It was here he met his future wife, Terry. She was eighteen years old at the time and played piano for the services.

After dating for two years, during which Jerry taught high schoolers in church and in general drew closer to the Lord, the couple married on April 12, 1957. Their marriage always included active church involvement wherever they were stationed, including beginning a small church in Germany, Faith

Baptist Church in Kaiserslautern, which today is one of the largest churches in the International Baptist Convention. It was here that Jerry was ordained as a Baptist deacon and continued teaching Bible studies, and Terry contributed her talents at the piano and organ and as a solo singer.

At this moment, as they prepared at the hotel to meet the president of the United States, their life together before Jerry's imprisonment seemed a million years past. Words could hardly express all the emotions Jerry was experiencing. He was still just getting used to being in the same room as his beautiful wife again. Before he was shot down, they had been married for eight wonderful years, enjoying each other and their two young children and Jerry's work in the military. As Jerry was fond of saying, "Life is good." Then disaster struck.

He was lost in recollections when Terry appeared in her evening gown, signaling she was ready. Jerry smiled as he remembered the first time he saw her at eighteen years old, playing the piano for a church revival service and wearing enormous orange flower earrings that covered half her cheeks. They stepped into the hallway of their hotel and rode the elevator downstairs. Attentive escorts pulled out huge umbrellas to protect them from the downpour that had persisted for the past thirty-six hours. The largest seated dinner ever held at the White House awaited them.

■ ■ ■

The evening was a blur for the Curtises. As Jerry and Terry joined the long reception line under a covered tunnel created to protect the arriving guests, Jerry relished seeing fellow POWs decked out in their crisp formal military attire. Everyone was polished and gleaming. He felt almost bewildered with joy.

Though the rain began to slacken, the White House lawn remained squishy wet. Attendants frantically covered the ground with burlap runners and straw, to little avail. Women, in a futile attempt to keep their skirts dry, hiked up their long evening dresses. Open-toed evening shoes sank down into soft, drenched turf, as did the legs of dining chairs. No one seemed to care. Someone even commented the downpour was God himself weeping tears of joy now that the POWs were home and out of the grasp of hell.

When President Nixon made it clear after dinner that they were welcome to roam through the White House unescorted, the guests became like kids in a candy store. Everyone agreed it was the highlight of the evening. One Navy pilot, shot down late in the war, afterward recalled exploring the upstairs with another former POW. Opening a door along an empty corridor, they walked in on the president himself, alone in his study. He simply waved, bidding them to make themselves at home.

The night continually offered surreal contrasts from the POWs' previous existence of years of imprisonment. The most important difference, of course, was exchanging captivity for freedom, delightfully demonstrated by their unfettered run of the White House.

But the differences abounded everywhere. They had exchanged chipped, glazed tin plates for historic fine china, stamped aluminum spoons for silver flatware, tin drinking cups for crystal flutes, and bowls of thin soup for as much sirloin steak au jus as they could eat. Even the tent itself presented a subtle contrast, its red and gold stripes seemingly morphed into a festive echo of the dingy red-and-beige striped prison pajamas worn 24-7 during their years within Hanoi's prison system.

Despite the lovely evening and its merriment, however, there would be long periods of adjustment ahead for nearly all returning POWs and their families. As ABC News White House correspondent Tom Jarriel pointed out during live television coverage of the event, some ninety returnees declined the White House dinner invitation for a host of different reasons. Some were still recuperating from various health issues, and some had met with devastating family news when they returned, such as wives who had died, leaving them widowers, or parents who were critically ill and required care. Others discovered themselves single again after spouses had obtained divorces in Mexico. A few returned with deep antiwar sentiments and declined the invitation as a form of protest. For many, adapting to the return home would prove as challenging as being away had been. For one, who took his life just nine days after the dinner party, the adjustment proved more difficult than could be endured.

Jerry looked down at the beautiful table setting before him. For 2,703 days, hunger had been his constant companion. Every man there that night had lost weight—forty, fifty, sixty pounds or more. He himself had, at his lowest point, weighed only 125 pounds. He had eaten scant bits of food, often riddled with worms or other foreign objects, always surrounded by gloom and darkness and the threat of torture. His journey to the splendor of a White House dinner had begun eight years previously at a remote outpost in Thailand, next to a little-known country bordered by a long river on one side and a winding trail on the other in a far-off corner of the world.

CHAPTER 2

NAKHON PHANOM

INDIAN HAWTHORNS CIRCLED by liriope already showed their spring foliage, and azaleas neared peak bloom across much of the Deep South on Sunday, March 21, 1965. In Selma, Alabama, over 3,200 demonstrators began a peaceful march toward Montgomery, the state capital, to protest voter discrimination. Baptist minister Dr. Martin Luther King Jr., at the head of the enormous crowd, began the walk by asking everyone to pray for him. It was a day marked with prayer across the nation as news of the event spread.

On that same day, the Curtises drove to church together for the last time before Jerry's departure for Thailand. A Baptist deacon, Jerry intended to solicit prayers from his church family for his own well-being. Since arriving at England Air Force

Base in Louisiana two years previously, he had functioned as detachment commander for local base rescue. Horseshoe Drive Baptist in nearby Alexandria served as his family's home church, and both Jerry and Terry found ways to serve.

Most of the congregation knew about Jerry's orders to Southeast Asia. And on his last Sunday, many made a point to seek him out with a promise to pray. Working his way to the children's area, he dropped off his four-year-old daughter, Lori, in the prekindergarten class and corralled his seven-year-old son, Tom, to the first graders' classroom.

Then the thirty-two-year-old captain headed toward a group of high school students he had taught for over a year to teach his final lesson. Once he finished, he closed his Bible, purposely leaving time to share about his circumstances.

"This is my last Sunday here as your teacher for a few months. As most of you know, I'm a pilot in the Air Force. I fly helicopters, and I've volunteered for a TDY assignment, which means temporary duty—120 days flying search and rescue in a war zone. So I'd like to ask you to pray for my wife, Terry, and our children. I'll need your prayers too—pray for me while I'm gone. I'll see you when I get back in the fall."

The teenagers listened quietly. Their teacher showed no outward anxiety, only his usual optimism.

Later, Jerry would admit he never realized what an enormous task he had relegated to them that morning, because by the time he returned to Horseshoe Drive Baptist Church in Alexandria, Louisiana—eight years later—these students had graduated from high school, finished college, found jobs, met future spouses, gotten married, and started families of their own.

. . .

Nakhon Phanom Royal Thai Air Force Base (NKP) became known as the "worst base in Thailand but the best we had in Vietnam." The latter accolade developed primarily because of three things, as the familiar real estate adage goes: "location, location, location." NKP sat about 5 miles from the Laotian border defined by the Mekong River, 75 miles from North Vietnam, and 230 miles, as the crow flies, from downtown Hanoi. Over its thirteen-year history, NKP would be involved in numerous major events in the war in Southeast Asia, including a variety of rescue and support missions.

But its ideal location could not overcome a quickly escalating conflict that caught the Air Force, according to respected military historian Earl H. Tilford Jr., with inadequate personnel, nonexistent doctrine, and ill-suited aircraft. Nowhere was the latter more evident than in the helicopters used for extracting downed crewmen from jungle terrain at the beginning of the war.

Built initially for US Navy at-sea rescues, the HH-43, known as the Huskie, primarily served the US Air Force in assisting firefighters, rescue crews, and personnel at crash sites. It was a serviceable machine for its original purpose. But in a war zone with a completely different type of rescue mission, it had three or four remarkable drawbacks, the most adverse being zero armor and zero armament.

Since space inside was limited, fixed machine guns couldn't be mounted to the floor. If a downed crewman needed to be air-evaced on a litter, every inch would be required. The crews themselves began carrying AR-15s, along with their .38 pistols.

To further complicate rescue efforts, hoist cables measured 100 feet. This was usually not long enough to reach the ground through the tall, dense jungle canopy, which often averaged over 125 feet in height.

These weren't the only limitations. The HH-43 had a top speed of about 120 knots. During a rescue attempt, however, it had to be slowed considerably throughout the entire process, mostly due to the extreme difficulty of spotting survivors in such heavily forested terrain. These helicopters became easy targets even for small-arms fire from below, and with a range radius of only seventy-five miles, the distance of missions across Laos and into Vietnam could push the helicopter's fuel capabilities to the limit.

When Jerry arrived in April 1965, the war was already ramping up, as was the importance of the NKP base. When Jerry was tapped to act as courier for top secret material at Travis AFB on his way over—handcuffed to a briefcase and wearing a holstered .45—it only served to emphasize he was headed to a war zone of increasing strategic importance.

As Jerry climbed out of the C-130 that had shuttled him from Bangkok to his new assignment at NKP, he walked past one of the pararescue jumpers. "Welcome to 'Naked Fanny,' sir," the young airman said. He was wearing a canvas safari hat with his flight suit sleeves rolled to the elbows, and he grinned as he gave Jerry a hasty salute.

These PJs, as they were called, were known for having a bit of an attitude, which served them well due to the dangerous elements of their mission. They rode the line down into the jungle to help airmen too wounded to help themselves. These well-trained paramedics could assess a person's condition, lend assistance, and tend to more extensive treatment once the wounded were hoisted into the choppers. The young PJ pointed Jerry toward the center of Nakhon Phanom Royal Thai Air Force Base, which was given the more memorable nickname "Naked Fanny" by previous American forces.

At this early point in the war, the outpost consisted primarily of a few dirt alleys flanked by wooden hooches with tin roofs. The door to one sported a torn piece of cardboard with a rabbit's head dressed in a black bow tie, hand drawn with colored markers. The sign read Officers' Club. Wooden sidewalks everywhere helped those stationed at the base to avoid mud during monsoon season. Later in the war, the base grew sizably as air traffic demands escalated.

But for now, three Huskies formed the extent of "firepower." Jerry walked over to where the "birds" were sitting. It didn't take much to see what the limitations were. In fact, one helicopter had a bullet hole in the Plexiglas between the rudders directly in front of the pilot's seat, just in case someone needed a reminder. A crew before his arrival had added pieces of quarter-inch steel in an attempt to reinforce the seats themselves. There was very little between the fliers in the air and the guns on the ground.

Despite the challenges and limitations, many downed crewmen already had been pulled from the jungle floor to safety, arriving back at NKP as if nothing untoward had happened. The rescued fliers owed their good fortune primarily to the sheer skill and courage of the Combat Search and Rescue (CSAR) crews to perform these missions.

After Jerry had been there for several weeks, he was eating lunch in the mess tent one day when a C-130 flew in. A fighter pilot got off the plane, then located Jerry. Placing a hand on his shoulder, the pilot said, "Thanks for my life." Jerry looked up to see one of the F-105 pilots he recently had rescued after the pilot had been shot down in the Savannakhet region of Laos.

"Great to see you again," said Jerry, "this time under better circumstances!"

"If it hadn't been for you, I might not be here now at all," the F-105 pilot said with a grin.

Jerry remembered the day of the rescue, when a Navy A-6 had been shot down near Tchepone, an area well-defended with antiaircraft artillery. A Marine helicopter had been launched to try to locate and rescue the two men but had to fly back for refueling before finding them.

In the meantime the F-105 pilot was returning to his base from a strike when he heard about the downed crew. The fighter pilot had decided to fly in and take a look. As he was coming out of the heavy clouds, he himself got shot down. Fortunately, he had been able to eject successfully, but now he also had found himself stranded in enemy territory.

It was at this point Jerry and his crew had been launched from NKP. "Do you remember how dicey the weather was that day?" Jerry asked the fighter pilot. "A couple of Navy A-1s radioed me and said if I could fly with them in formation, they thought they could take me to where you were."

"Yeah, I remember you told me that. I'm sure glad they got you to me," said the fighter pilot, "or else I'd still be there!"

Jerry thought about flying into Laos to rescue the man standing in front of him now. "When we got to where they thought you were, I looked down and saw a large village. That was a gut-wrenching moment—I had no idea what to expect from that point forward," said Jerry, remembering it had been impossible to know whether there might be antiaircraft artillery in villages or other ground fire from enemy soldiers hiding among the buildings.

"I spotted that clearing and decided to chance it. I told my crew chief just to haul you in when he got his hands on you," laughed Jerry, who had come down to a five-foot hover, never touching the ground so they could take off as soon as the downed pilot was hustled on board.

"Man, when I saw your chopper coming down, I've never been so glad to see anything in my life," said the fighter pilot. "I ran like crazy and just jumped up—your mechanic grabbed me and pulled me in!"

They both enjoyed reminiscing about the successful rescue mission. Before he left, he reached over and shook Jerry's hand once more. "Thanks again. I'll never forget you."

Jerry watched the F-105 pilot exit the mess hall. Such a moment made all risk to his own life worthwhile.

Saving American lives, however, didn't comprise the only rescue missions Jerry participated in at NKP. One day an emergency call came in from Udorn Royal Thai Air Force Base in northern Thailand. Help was needed in assisting a very wealthy Thai family who had been assaulted while traveling in their vehicle.

"We've got a call for assistance to some locals who've been robbed—and I'll need one of the PJs to come along," Jerry announced to his crew. He hurriedly directed them to their helicopter and then flew about twenty minutes to a deserted north-south highway. As he approached the area, he made a tricky landing between two fences on the narrow road paved with laterite pebbles. Several Thai policemen were already there.

"What have we got?" Jerry approached quickly and saw a man lying on the ground.

"Man shot. Can you take to hospital?" The policeman led Jerry over to where some family members were pacing anxiously, some kneeling beside their wounded relative. In Thailand, wealth often is displayed by gold—usually in the form of personal jewelry—and lots of it. The shine creates an enticing target.

On this particular occasion, robbers had run down the car, and during the heist, they shot the patriarch of the family for resisting. Though the man was conscious, it looked like a very serious wound judging from the amount of blood on his clothing and the pavement.

Jerry motioned immediately for his crew to carry the injured man to the chopper. In moments they were airborne again, flying the senior Thai gentleman to Udorn for medical attention. Meanwhile, Jerry's PJ began attending the man's wounds.

But before Jerry had left the scene, the other Thai family members expressed heartfelt thanks for his help, embracing him and touching his arms. This was not the only time Jerry experienced the gratitude of the people of Thailand.

On one assignment, he also learned how they viewed important symbols of liberty. One of Jerry's missions in-country was to fly explosive ordinance disposal teams into remote areas to check for unexploded bombs. Usually flight surgeons went along to hold "sick calls"—a way of offering treatment to the Thai living in nearby villages. These sick calls resulted in families bringing their children for free exams.

While the surgeons tended to patients, Jerry used the time on the ground to pass out little wrapped candies to the children.

On this occasion, he had numerous small American flags on wooden sticks to hand out as well.

Jerry always had enjoyed having children around him. On this day, he thought of his own kids back home, four and seven years old, and wondered what they were doing. He missed them.

The pilot was having a wonderful time passing out candy and flags when one of the older Thai men hurried up to him. He began yanking the flags out of the children's hands. Jerry at first thought the man might object to the American symbol for some reason. But when he asked why he took away the flags, the man's answer caught him by surprise.

"These not toys . . . these not to play with . . . these important, not toys." The man held the small flags proudly. From then on, Jerry reserved the American flags for the adults and passed out just candy to the children.

The landscape and people in Thailand were exotic and beautiful. Jerry relished times he could participate in any way possible to either deliver assistance to the Thai or create good public relations. His trips into neighboring Laos, however, were remarkable also . . . but for completely different reasons.

CHAPTER 3

THE SECRET WAR IN LAOS

SUMMER 1965

DURING HIS TIME AT NKP, Jerry flew in and out of Laos with increasing frequency as the importance of this country lodged between Thailand and Vietnam became more evident. CIA operatives established clandestine military bases, small at first, where Laotian forces friendly to US interests could hook up with rescue missions, covert military operations, and any endeavors connected to the war effort. These bases came to be called Lima Sites with a simple numerical designation.

One of the most important Lima Sites was LS98, also known as LS20A or Long Tieng. The CIA established the base in 1962 primarily as headquarters for Vang Pao, a two-star general in the Royal Lao Army and commander of the Hmong guerrilla forces. He was already well on his way to becoming a legend in that part of the world for his bravery and commitment to fighting Communist forces intent on taking over Laos. His desire to see the forces of North Vietnam defeated made him a natural ally for the United States.

Lima Site 98 expanded quickly and by the late sixties contained a long runway, which some called the busiest airport in the world. Forty thousand inhabitants made it the second largest city in Laos, although it appeared on no maps, giving rise to another label, the "most secret place on earth." It was located 3,100 feet above sea level, surrounded by mountains with a steep karst, or large limestone outcropping, at one end of the runway. These geographical features provided natural defenses in an already remote area.

On Jerry's initial trip into Lima Site 98, he was ordered to fly through Udorn Royal Thai Air Force Base first in order to pick up someone who needed a lift to the post in Laos. Shortly after Jerry set down his helicopter at Udorn, a stocky American man strode across the runway, a carbine loosely slung across his shoulder and a dog-eared Ian Fleming paperback sticking out of the pocket of his blue jeans. He quickly jumped into Jerry's helicopter and said, "Thanks for the lift. So this is your first time to LS98?" His gravelly voice was memorable.

"Yes, it is. I've heard about the karst at the end of the runway. And that you can get a lot of weather there," Jerry said. Before leaving NKP, he had been told only that he was picking up an American government worker who had business at Lima Site 98. The new passenger stretched out his large hand toward Jerry's extended handshake and said, "You probably won't be able to pronounce my last name either—most people just call me Tony Poe. If you need me, I can help out navigating visually."

"That'd be fine," said Jerry. "I've had reports of the topographical features that make takeoff and landing somewhat exciting, even under optimum conditions."

But as they flew into Laos, the weather turned nasty. Cloud cover completely enveloped the region below them for miles. Jerry, on dead reckoning, radioed the base.

"This is Pedro 1 calling Lima Site 98. We are above the overcast, inbound for Lima 98."

Almost immediately, an Air America pilot called back. "Not a problem. . . . I'll come up to get you and bring you down."

In just a few minutes, Jerry saw an H-34 helicopter appear as if by magic on top of the clouds, having emerged not far from where he was flying. The pilot had come up through a "sucker hole," an opening in the overcast that, if a flyer is willing to gamble, can be used to get through the clouds to the ground. The problem is that these openings can close up just as soon as they open—hence the name "sucker hole."

Before he could analyze the situation further, the H-34 ducked back into the "hole." Immediately, Jerry joined the H-34 and followed him down into the thick clouds. Continually circling, the two helicopters finally came out from the overcast not far from the looming karst. The runway was just below them. Jerry hovered for a second and lightly landed.

"Welcome to Lima 98," said Tony Poe, grinning. He gave Jerry a hearty slap on the back and bounced out of the helicopter.

In the succeeding days, Jerry found colorful people matched the exotic sights and landscape of this remote base. And one of the most interesting turned out to be the passenger to whom he had given a ride.

Tony Poe, short for Poshepny, was a CIA operative working

undercover in Southeast Asia, especially Laos, to organize and lead guerrilla forces fighting against the Communists. His reputation was growing by the week—some said he often filled large manila envelopes with actual ears cut off enemy combatants when authorities in Washington questioned his numerical assessments of defeated soldiers. He lived on a large farm just on the outskirts of LS98 and had married a woman some said was a Laotian princess.

Jerry saw him often when he flew into the remote area, and Tony Poe, grateful for rides when he needed them, kept Jerry and his crews supplied with bushels of roasting ears he himself had grown on his farm. Tony would fill several large baskets and have his children deliver them to the helicopter pilot. On each successive trip into the site, Jerry and his crews ate fresh corn for breakfast, lunch, and dinner, dipping the hot cobs down into gallon buckets of butter labeled USDA.

On days when he wasn't flying missions, Jerry enjoyed spending time walking through a large area of open-air market stalls selling everything from Singha beer to opium. People dressed in a variety of gear wandered through the maze of tables. Tribal soldiers in military garb, Hmong fighters in more traditional uniforms, Thai mercenaries in camouflage fatigues, and CIA operatives dressed in jeans and T-shirts all milled about among native Laotians who had come from surrounding villages to sell their wares.

One morning when he was there with his crew chief, gunshots rang out, always cause for alarm in a war zone. "Get behind this table!" Jerry yelled at his crewmate. They crouched down, not knowing what might happen next until they learned a villager had sold a water buffalo that was on the hoof. The villager shot it and immediately began butchering the enormous animal on the spot. As Jerry carefully rounded the corner of one of the stalls, he saw a Laotian who had just bought an entire hindquarter scurrying off with his fresh meat thrown over his shoulders, buffalo leg and all.

The reality was that the site was more Wild West than military base. Contract pilots flew a variety of planes in and out of the site, the steep karst at one end of the runway testing the skills of even the most daring. One pilot enjoyed taking off with his window down, beating on the side of the airplane with his cowboy hat as if urging it up and over the high limestone outcropping like a bucking bronco. As a Texas son with a love for Western US history who had spent many Sunday afternoons with friends trying to ride anything that could buck in his family's corral, Jerry found the sights and sounds of Long Tieng strangely familiar, if not exhilarating.

It wasn't long before Jerry met several contract pilots who flew for Air America, the CIA-sponsored group helping to establish bases throughout Laos. On one of his trips there, weather kept him from continuing on to his final destination of LS36 to assist in establishing an HH-43 operation at that site. He decided to ask one of the Air America pilots if he could go along on a supply delivery trip into the remote mountainous areas.

"Sure," said the pilot, "great to have you." So Jerry climbed into the H-34, which was ready to take off.

After they were airborne, Jerry realized the entire helicopter was heavily loaded with all sorts of supplies for the remote drops. There was also one young Filipino riding in the back. As they flew along, the pilot explained the procedure.

"We pack the chopper with as much as we can get into it. Because the site is at a high altitude, we can't do a hover landing."

Jerry still wasn't exactly sure how they were going to accomplish the delivery, but it became clear after they reached the first mountain site. Once the pilot arrived at the target area, he made slow passes back and forth above the drop zone. The Filipino literally began kicking the durable supplies out the door of the helicopter. Included in the supplies were sacks of rice, double bagged, since impact often broke open the inner bags.

This continued until the chopper's weight was reduced enough to execute a hover landing. Finally, the Air America pilot set down, and Jerry helped the two men unload the remaining supplies.

It turned out the pilot was supplying a Laotian family known as a "road-watch team." These scouts for the CIA kept track of who was coming up and down the trails and alerted them when any troop movement or matériel was spotted.

The weather had been overcast with very low, thick clouds for several days but finally lifted, and Jerry and his crew were able to continue on to the extremely high Lima site known as LS36. Once they landed, a special forces officer invited all of the HH-43 crews for lunch.

"Let's go over to the mess hall and see if there's anything we can find to eat," he suggested to the helicopter pilot.

"Sounds great to me," said Jerry.

The special forces officer led them to a large wooden hooch with open sides. Here, several long-planked tables were located in the shady interior, and on top of one Jerry saw a huge black mound in the middle. Coming in from the bright sunlight, he couldn't quite make out what it was, but as he approached it, he realized the entire surface was moving.

When Jerry reached the table, suddenly the mound turned white as thousands of flies flew away with a distinct buzzing sound. Underneath, to his disbelief, were several pounds of cooked rice that had been dumped into the center of the table for serving. When someone wanted something to eat, he just went over and carved out his portion. Somehow kickers and black rice seemed to fit in with everything else Jerry was learning about this remote corner of the world.

■ ■ ■

Initially, all American planes and soldiers traveling in and out of these Lima sites bore no identifying insignias or markings on either their clothing or the planes. Jerry and his crew, along with one other rescue unit from NKP, were the very first to fly into Lima Site 98 with United States Air Force markings on their equipment and uniforms. General Vang Pao, elated to have these significant symbols of alliance with the United States clearly visible in his headquarters, wasted no time in planning an elaborate celebration in honor of the US airmen.

Vang Pao, or VP as some people called him, commanded the Hmong guerrilla forces, known for their fierce fighting and loyalty to the general. After the war, Vang Pao settled in the United States, a hero to thousands of Asians who sought refuge here after the war, especially to the Laotians living mainly in the northwest. For them, Vang Pao was larger than life, a walking legend in their midst whom they revered and continued to honor with their allegiance.

On Jerry's first trip to Lima 98, the general sent his body-guard, an imposing-looking soldier whose face had been badly disfigured by a bear, to inform Tony Poe of the invitation, who in turn informed Jerry and the other American crews. Escorted to a more secluded area of the camp, the airmen reached a large pavilion shaded by canvases stretched above a wooden floor with open sides and rails around its edges. The platform sat several feet above the ground. As Jerry's crew and one other arrived, the general motioned for the officers to be seated cross-legged on the floor in a semicircle, with enlisted men standing behind.

Tables laden with all sorts of foods and fruit lined one side of the pavilion. Very shortly afterward, someone switched on a power generator, and three Laotian young men cranked up electric guitars with several speakers booming. About twenty young girls dressed in traditional Laotian apparel began swinging to the music, performing native dances and also their interpretation of Western steps.

After dining and entertainment, the ceremony took a more serious turn. Signaling for quiet, General Vang Pao motioned everyone to be seated. He approached Jerry and the other Americans with instructions. "Hold out hands," he said, motioning for them to place their palms up. After a few words of gratitude for their alliance, spoken in broken English, he tied a white string around Jerry's left arm, a Laotian symbol of friendship and blessing. Then the general placed a small boiled egg in one hand and a shot glass filled to the brim with Johnnie Walker scotch in the other.

As a general rule, Jerry refrained from drinking any kind of alcohol. Two primary reasons motivated this abstinence. First, his position as a deacon in the Baptist church mandated a "no drinking" policy. But the second reason probably held a tighter grip on him than conservative Christian beliefs did: his father customarily drenched rock candy with alcohol whenever the children had sore throats growing up, and the smell, from that point forward, was obnoxious to Jerry: it always reminded him of being sick.

The situation posed a distinct dilemma. In Eastern cultures, it is considered extremely impolite to refuse to eat and drink what a host offers. And in this case, the delight of the general and other Laotian dignitaries for their American allies added to the awkwardness of declining. Not wanting to offend his gracious host, he ate the egg and gulped down the scotch. Then the next dignitary stepped up, tied a string around his wrist, placed a cookie in one hand, and filled the shot glass in the other . . . again to the brim. Jerry obliged once more.

After another dignitary came forward, the pilot noticed they were switching from scotch to a drink called Lao Lao, a distilled fiery brew made from sticky rice, the Laotian version of white lightning. The third dignitary in line tied another string of friendship around his wrist, placed a piece of food in one hand, and filled his shot glass to the brim with Lao Lao. The pilot ate and drank. This time, however, the alcohol nearly took his breath away. Many of the other Americans either snorted or wheezed as they swigged down the Asian moonshine.

When Jerry caught his breath, he looked up to see at least eighteen more officials standing in line with their string, their hors d'oeuvres, and their lethal liquid. He realized he was in trouble. If he rejected their offerings, it would be viewed as an insult to the Laotians' generous hospitality. But to continue downing these full shots of straight, potent alcohol surely would produce equally dire results.

Faced with a mounting dilemma and trying to find a graceful way out, he looked down between his crossed legs, where a small knothole in the wooden floor about the size of a quarter caught his eye. He suddenly remembered a line from the Lord's Prayer and gave a quick word of thanks for being led away from temptation. He raised the next shot glass to his lips, then quickly lowered it discreetly between his legs, pouring the contents through the hole onto the ground below.

The others, however, must not have found any knotholes. At the end of the evening, most weaved their way off the platform, some struggling more than others. One airman had to be half carried, half dragged back to his sleeping quarters. But none of them would ever forget the friendship ceremony of the strings. And Jerry kept the dozens of white threads representing blessings from General Vang Pao and the other Laotian officials tied around his left arm.

■ ■ ■

The charismatic two-star general was not the only Royal Lao Armed Forces leader Jerry worked with while in Southeast Asia. Late one afternoon, an urgent message came in from Udorn requesting emergency assistance in Laos. Royal Lao regulars had been ambushed by Pathet Lao forces, resulting in a bloody skirmish that left many wounded. Jerry flew to a Laotian base, where he was met by the commander of the Laotian Air Force.

One-star general Thao Ma explained to Jerry and his crew that several severely injured soldiers needed to be air-evacuated, but the battle had taken place in an isolated area with extremely rough terrain. A Laotian navigator, who ironically had just returned to Laos after being trained in Waco, Texas, told the American pilot he thought he could direct him to the location.

They headed out with the navigator seated next to Jerry, flying deeper and deeper into a remote section of jungle thick with enemy troops. After arriving in the vicinity where they thought the emergency call had come from, they spotted soldiers signaling from the ground. When Jerry landed the helicopter, he discovered the fighters had triaged the wounded, separating the men they thought had the best chance of surviving. The other unharmed soldiers planned to evacuate the area as soon as the helicopter took off, leaving to certain death those left behind.

The area seemed eerily quiet, almost surreal. As Jerry walked through the men on the ground, the only sounds were the muffled moans of men in great pain and suffering. He made a quick decision—he wouldn't leave any of them. He instructed his crew to cover the back of the helicopter with a large poncho, and they motioned for the Laotians to begin loading all who were injured. In order to get everybody on the small floor space, they had to stack all thirteen or fourteen men like cordwood. Most were bleeding profusely; some were already unconscious. They moved as rapidly as possible, since enemy forces might break through at any moment.

Once airborne again, Jerry flew directly back to the airfield in Savannakhet, Laos, where several ambulances waited to carry the wounded to a nearby hospital fully equipped for surgery and whatever other medical services might be required. After the Laotian soldiers were unloaded, he returned to his helicopter and stopped, staring at the poncho on the floor. Two of his men came up behind and looked over his shoulder. Without saying a word, he motioned his crew inside the chopper. Together the three men lifted the poncho up at its corners—huge puddles of still-warm blood flowed to the ground outside. It was the captain's first real look at what ground war was all about.

Jerry's tour of duty was supposed to be temporary—just 120 days. He had volunteered knowing that an assignment to Southeast Asia would come regardless. But at the end of four months, Jerry's tour was extended another sixty days as the military continued to solidify personnel and aircraft in Thailand. It was a disappointment but not entirely unexpected.

Jerry's wife, Terry, remained in Louisiana with their children. They were living in the same home close to England AFB, continuing with all their school and church activities. Jerry called Terry to give her the news of the extension. The overseas telephone connection was poor, with static and delays, so they talked only briefly. It was the last they would hear the sound of each other's voices for seven and a half years. Just twenty days before his scheduled return home, the event that would forever alter his life—and that of his family—occurred without any premonition at all.

CHAPTER 4

THE SHOOT-DOWN

SEPTEMBER 20, 1965

WHEN THE EMERGENCY ALERT came in shortly past noon on September 20, 1965, Captain Jerry Curtis and his crew—1st Lieutenant Duane Martin, copilot; Airman First Class Bill Robinson, crew chief; and Airman Third Class Neil Black, pararescue jumper—immediately began rescue-operation preparations. An Air Force F-105 had been shot down just beyond the Laotian border in North Vietnam. The fighter's wingman observed the pilot ejecting, then remained in the area until he had received a "good beep" from the ground, a radio signal confirming the downed pilot was still alive and where he was located.

Jerry and his copilot, Martin, quickly scanned wall maps to locate the area where the downed airman was presumed to be. After calculating heading and distance, they called for an additional barrel of fuel to be loaded onto the helicopter. Enterprising crews before them had developed a way of carrying extra fuel in fifty-five-gallon barrels. As the pilots charted the mission route, they would call for an additional one, two, or three barrels, depending on how far they had to fly. When a barrel was emptied, the crew chiefs simply pushed it out the back of the helicopter, their personal contribution to the "bombing" effort.

Jerry grabbed his clipboard and held the door of the radar hooch open. "We'll be flying low bird for this one. Robinson will be operating hoist." Helicopter rescue missions normally used two helicopters in their recovery efforts, one flying high bird as backup, one flying low bird to pick up the downed airman.

The four-man HH-43 crew ran to board their waiting helicopter, call sign "Dutchy 41," and strapped in. In the meantime, two A-1 Skyraiders, nicknamed Spads, staging out of NKP and operating under the call sign "Sandy," also readied for takeoff heading toward the same location. Since the HH-43s carried no firepower, their missions were accompanied by two of these planes. They held 20mm cannons and folding fin rockets and could provide formidable firepower, keeping enemy ground forces down while the helicopter worked to complete the rescue.

"All right. Let's go get our guy and bring him back home for supper." Jerry's voice, as usual, was calm and confident. Seconds later, the long counter-rotating rotors began their steadily increasing staccato whirls, and the helicopter lunged upward and forward. The Mekong River lay just ahead.

Flying loose formation with the second helicopter in a generally northward heading, the pilot soon found himself over extremely rugged Laotian terrain. Scattered emergent trees towered above an already high jungle canopy, creating a near-solid green blanket some 3,500 feet beneath the rescue helicopter. As they approached the projected crash site, Jerry spotted the two escort Spads circling.

"This is Dutchy 41. What have you got for me?"

"We've picked up a clear signal from the ground, but tree coverage is really thick here," the A-1 pilot radioed back.

Jerry began the usual methodical searching in a slow hover as his crew continued to scrutinize the area for signs: debris, smoke—anything that would help them identify the exact location. Suddenly, a pistol flare pierced upward through the forest canopy, and Jerry maneuvered the helicopter toward it. Small arms fire could be heard from several different directions.

"Okay, Robbie, talk to me," said Jerry. Using "hot mics," the pilot and his crew chief now began the tedious process of working together to execute the rescue mission. Bill Robinson would have to be the "eyes" of his pilot since the tree canopy below was so thick, Jerry couldn't see anything at all on the ground. Maneuvering to avoid nicking the treetops with the chopper's blades required his total attention.

When Robinson leaned out over the edge of the open door, wind ripping past, he could hear bullets pelting the sides of the helicopter. Suddenly, he spotted the downed pilot through the trees.

"I've got a visual, Captain. Come back left a little . . . okay, okay. . . . I've got a visual. Come right now, come right a bit. A little forward . . . okay . . . steady . . . steady . . . I'm lowering the hoist . . . hoist going down." Bill began to run out the line.

Jerry continued hovering, with Bill calling out necessary

adjustments in position so that the hoist could be lowered as close as possible to the downed pilot. The crew chief, by now, could see him clearly on the ground.

What happened next, however, made an already grave situation suddenly worse. Jerry glanced upward to see black plumes billowing from one of the escort Spads.

"I'm hit! I'm hit!" signaled the A-1 pilot as smoke continued to pour from the rocket pod. After repeating another emergency call, the pilot banked off to fly back to Thailand. The second escort plane, which normally would have continued to provide cover for Jerry's helicopter, also broke off to shadow the other plane back to base. These A-1 crews had been trained to return together as a unit when they flew as attack bombers, but now, in their new capacity of escorting unarmed helicopters, one should have remained behind to provide cover for Jerry's helicopter.

In the years following, Jerry never blamed them for leaving the area. His explanation was simple: "This was how they normally would have done their job; assisting rescue helicopters was, unfortunately, just not on their learning curve yet."

Now, the unarmed HH-43 was alone and completely vulnerable. But Jerry stayed, continuing to push down into the treetops to give his crew chief the best possible chance of delivering a lifeline to the man they were trying to rescue.

"We're right on top of him. . . . We're almost there . . ." Bill said into his mic as he noticed he had red line in his hands. The cable extended one hundred feet in length, with the last ten feet painted red to alert the hoist operator how much more remained. He immediately relayed the information to the pilot.

Jerry pushed the fuselage down into the treetops to give the downed pilot a better chance of reaching the hoist.

"He's got the hoist! He's got it!" the crew chief called to his pilot. Jerry recognized two things happening almost simultaneously—a difference in weight indicating the pilot was on the hoist and off the ground . . . and a quick burst of ground fire.

At this point, the rotor blades were no more than a foot or so above the treetops. As he tried to take the helicopter upward, when there should have been 100 percent power, suddenly he had power failure. Within seconds, the Huskie's large, whirling rotors began nicking leaves and branches, creating thousands of toothpicks out of its laminated blades.

Fortunately, the thickness of the canopy kept the helicopter from over-ending, an event that would have resulted in certain death for its occupants. Instead, it stayed upright and fell flat but very hard and fast through the trees. Jerry's last thoughts before crashing were for the pilot on the hoist.

Lord, please don't let me kill this man by landing on top of him.

Upon impact, all four crewmen hurriedly clawed their way out of the helicopter. They knew it would soon be overrun with enemy soldiers. The force of the landing resulted in hairline fractures in Robinson's neck plus jamming of his kneecaps—he had been kneeling while operating the hoist.

When Jerry reached down to pull out his M16, which he kept wedged between his door and seat, he found that the stock had broken from the violent fall. As he leaned over to get out the door, Jerry realized his spinal column had been jarred severely during the hard one-hundred-foot drop—he experienced a sudden bolt of very sharp pain below his waist and suspected he had sustained some kind of compression injury. But adrenaline was kicking in, and for the moment, his survival instinct took precedence.

God . . . help us survive this day . . .

Jerry looked around for his copilot, who seemed completely disoriented for a moment. In his excitement while trying to get out of his parachute, Duane Martin had nearly shot himself in the foot with his own weapon.

As they huddled together in front of the crash, Jerry spotted the downed fighter pilot they had been trying to rescue. He ran over to him. "Hey—Tom Curtis—are you all right?" Jerry helped the pilot scramble out of the hoist and up on his feet.

"Yeah—Will Forby—I think I'm okay," answered the pilot.

Jerry knew all the antennas located on the bottom of the helicopter would be useless for signaling the second chopper. He immediately reached for a small handheld radio. Much to his disappointment, when he pulled it out of his flight suit, he discovered its antenna was also broken.

"Come on," he yelled to his men. "Let's get away from this crash site." Enemy troops certainly would lose no time getting to them. They could hide until dark, then maybe get back to a safer area. Jerry, Neil Black, and Bill Robinson half ran, half slid down a nearby steep ravine, then across a muddy stream and started back up the other side. They all thought Duane Martin and the downed fighter pilot were following along behind them.

As they scurried upward through dense forest growth, the three men reached an enormous fallen tree with a huge trunk covered with thick vegetation about two-thirds of the way up to the top of the ridge. They immediately crawled behind and under it as much as they could.

Jerry looked around and didn't see Martin.

"Where's Duane?" he whispered to his other two crewmen.

"Don't know, sir," said Robinson, breathing hard. "Looks like the other pilot is somewhere back behind us too."

They hunkered down at the sound of shots in the distance. *Oh, God . . . don't let them find us . . .*

Moments later, they heard the second helicopter flying somewhere above them and, almost simultaneously, small arms fire began coming from somewhere nearby in the jungle. Jerry looked up—it was directly over them.

He quickly set off a pencil flare. But when he heard the helicopter being pummeled with bullets, he waved it away, knowing that any second it, too, might be shot down if they stayed. Jerry thought he had done an unselfish act until he learned, years later, the other crew never saw him through the thick foliage.

He then ducked back down behind the log. Within twenty minutes or so, they heard loud thrashing noises through the brush, men shouting back and forth.

Jerry peeked over the top of the log. In the distance he could make out thirty or forty men armed with a variety of weapons and deduced they were militia. He reached down and yanked off the strings he still wore on his left arm, tied by the two-star Laotian general Vang Pao and other dignitaries at the friendship ceremony of strings. He didn't have any desire to try and explain what they were to these Vietnamese soldiers.

At first he thought they might even sweep past where he and his crew were hiding, but as soon as the Vietnamese were directly down the slope from where they were, several turned, hastened up the ravine, and stumbled almost on top of them. They quickly yelled for the others, and a huge crowd of angry men suddenly pointed everything from machetes to automatic weapons down upon the faces of the airmen.

Jerry had long before decided he would not try to fight a war with a .38 pistol, the extent of firepower he had left after losing his M16 during the crash. It wouldn't have made any difference. The three men were overpowered by arms and numbers.

Reluctantly, he stood up. The other two crewmen followed suit, and within seconds they were tied up, elbows and wrists pulled tightly behind their backs. Neither Duane Martin nor the fighter pilot Will Forby were anywhere to be seen.

Ropes of imprisonment now replaced the strings of friendship. And just that unceremoniously, Captain Thomas "Jerry" Curtis found himself a captive of war.

CHAPTER 5

HEARTBREAK HOTEL

SEPTEMBER–OCTOBER 1965

THREE DAYS BEFORE Captain Thomas "Jerry" Curtis was shot down in North Vietnam, CBS aired the first episode of a brand-new series depicting life in a German POW camp during World War II. It was an instant success. *Hogan's Heroes* amused audiences for years with its bungling guard, Schultz, attempting to manage the antics of his resident captives. Life as a prisoner of war looked playful and mischievously challenging. Reality, on the other hand, was something entirely different.

The initial trauma of capture by enemy soldiers created a sense of intense alertness—Jerry remained calm, yet at the same time every nerve in his body was taut. Though these militia members seemed somewhat disorganized and anxious themselves, their intentions were obvious. The Americans would not be allowed to communicate with one another and would be kept separated at all costs.

Immediately after Jerry's hands and arms were tied tightly behind his back, a group of a dozen or so men began marching him into the jungle. The other two members of his crew also were bound and, as far as he could determine, were being taken in the same general direction.

Once he began to travel with this armed militia, he had a few moments to gather his thoughts.

Please, Lord, keep us safe. Help us live through this day . . .

After a couple of hours, they reached a small village, and Jerry was placed inside a hut, alone and still bound. He stretched out on the wooden floor to catch his breath. Pain riveted through his back. It was then he realized how badly he was injured.

Suddenly several men burst into the hut and motioned for him to get up. They pushed Jerry outside, and angry villagers began yelling at him. At first their protests were limited to shouting and shaking fists, but soon someone picked up a rock and threw it. Then several others followed suit, and quickly he was being pelted with anything they could find to throw. He tried to keep his head down to protect his eyes.

As the crowd's fury escalated, several of the Vietnamese soldiers grabbed him by the arms and shoved him back into the hut. Jerry sat down again, exhausted.

It took about a week for the North Vietnamese to transport their American prizes to Hanoi. Traveling at night and sleeping during the day, the militia shoved the captives from one small village to the next. Once, Jerry was fairly certain he caught a glimpse of the fighter pilot they had been trying to rescue, but he couldn't be sure.

In each village where they stopped, a local commissar incited residents to near rioting, and they attacked Jerry with rocks, sticks, bamboo rods—anything they could use as weapons. Some would dart at him punching and kicking before the guards halfheartedly waved them away.

At this point, Jerry felt more bewildered than anything, though deep fatigue began to set in. It didn't take long to realize his legs were not in the kind of shape needed to traverse rough, steep terrain all night, especially with hands tied behind his back preventing the use of his arms for balance. His back now produced severe pain with every step. Branches, leaves, and thick jungle foliage continually slapped across his face. By the third day, he was tattered and sticky with cuts and sweat.

Whenever he was loaded onto a truck, he was blindfolded first. If he sensed one of his men might be near him inside the vehicle, he tried to whisper, "Are you okay?" But guards reacted quickly to squash any attempts to communicate with blows to his head or back.

Eventually the militia turned him over to North Vietnamese army regulars. These uniformed, more professional soldiers loaded him onto an open-backed truck that continued northward over dirt roads filled with potholes. One night they crossed a river with Jerry forced to lie flat on the bottom of a small boat, hands and feet both tied. He listened to the sounds of water slapping the side of the boat and prayed he would survive the night.

It was on this night that the helplessness of the situation began to crystallize in his mind. When they reached villages, he was given a little rice during each day, the only time his hands were free. His mouth was completely dry—he was accustomed to drinking lots of water, and right then he would have given anything for a cold jug of it.

After a few days, Jerry's growing sense of anxiety centered mainly around his inability to determine who of his crew was near or whether the pilot they had been attempting to rescue was in the group. These regular army soldiers did an even better job than the militia of keeping him isolated from his crew. As their commander, he felt responsible for all of them—he hated not knowing their whereabouts. With every passing day, the Communists of North Vietnam reinforced a primary goal: to keep their American prisoners feeling helpless and alone.

■ ■ ■

The jostling in the back of the truck smoothed out. Jerry surmised they were now traveling on semipaved streets. Even though it was nighttime, he thought he could detect muffled city noises along the way.

He was trying to decide how many days it had been since his capture—he guessed at least a week—when the vehicle came to an abrupt stop. He heard the sound of large, heavy gates creaking open, then the truck rolling forward over what felt from the vibrations like cobblestones. Afterward thick doors slammed shut somewhere behind him.

Guards pulled him down from the truck and marched him across an open area into what seemed like the interior of a building. Before he knew it, he was shoved into a very small cell, and at last his captors removed the blindfold. A short, uniformed guard wearing a pith helmet motioned for him to undress and handed him a pair of thin cotton pajama-style pants with a drawstring waist and a loose-fitting shirt, both pieces red-and-beige striped. So far, not a single person had spoken a word of English.

While he changed clothes, the guards confiscated his flight suit, boots, watch, and dog tags. The only things of his own he was left with were his socks and underwear. As he dressed in his prison clothes, he quickly noticed the tight space contained two narrow concrete slabs. The ceiling seemed exceptionally high, with a bare lightbulb hanging out of reach from the ceiling, which Jerry soon learned burned continuously. The room smelled sour, rank with putrid, acidic odors. All its dark gray surfaces looked dingy and oppressive.

As he handed over his belongings to the guards, he observed iron stocks embedded in the concrete at the foot of both slabs. The rusty manacles with their long, formidable bars appeared too old to be serviceable. Jerry decided they couldn't possibly be functional anymore, a deduction he would find false in the days to come. The guard spun around, banging the door shut behind him. Jerry heard keys scraping the rusty lock . . . then complete silence.

The world knew this dungeon-like structure as Maison Centrale, the formal name French occupiers used for it. Built over several years and completed in 1898, then added onto later, it occupied an entire city block in the center of Hanoi, North Vietnam. The Vietnamese name, Hoa Lo, meant "Fiery Furnace," a reference to the street on which the prison was located, a street known for its pottery shops with goods fired in kilns.

But the name also represented the hellish existence of those unfortunate enough to be manacled in its grasp. The prison's storied past included accounts of torture chambers within dark interiors and ranked high in the annals of brutality and abuse of prisoners. It had earned its reputation as being the Devil's Island of Southeast Asia. Death and despair seemed to permeate every corner, a "fiery furnace" indeed for the ill-fated souls who entered its gates.

The French had built the compound as a maximum-security prison to allow little, if any, possibility of escape. Fifteen- to twenty-foot-high walls topped with broken-glass fragments and barbed wire surrounded the compound filled with dark, filthy cells, many of them hardly large enough to turn around in. Over the years, most high window openings within the cells, which might have allowed an occasional wisp of outside air to enter, had been covered with woven fiber mats, creating interiors that often topped 110 degrees during the summer months, even at midnight. Because the prison was constructed mostly of concrete, the reverse was true in winter months—the thermometer dropped to cold, even frigid temperatures.

This enormous prison complex in downtown Hanoi contained a series of buildings divided into sections of various configurations. In the area of the prison often used to confine men when they were first captured, tiny cells housed usually a single occupant. Since Jerry had been blindfolded until he was shoved into his cell, he had managed only peeks out from under its edges.

Tired to the bone, partly from physical exhaustion, partly from hunger, the airman lay alone in the stone closet, his six-foot athletic frame completely filling the cement slab. He closed his eyes.

The past week swirled in his mind—an avalanche of thoughts coming one on top of another. The trauma of crashing, of hiding, of being tied up, of angry mobs hitting and yelling, of enemy soldiers beating, jabbing with their rifles, of the pain in his back—he felt numb and hyper at the same time.

What will Terry do when she finds out? Help her, God. Help both of us . . .

Jerry knew it might take months for military authorities to know for sure what had happened to him. Jerry prayed for his family.

Finally, one thought surfaced above all the others, and the event that would forever define his life began to sink in: he was a million miles from home, locked in a North Vietnamese prison, a prisoner of war.

His exhausted mind allowed only a few more coherent thoughts before slipping over the edge into oblivion.

God, I hope my crew made it okay, and the pilot we were trying to rescue.

The bare, glaring lightbulb did nothing more to hinder sleep, which quickly overcame him that first night.

But after several hours, Jerry jerked awake, the nightmare of his situation engulfing him again. He sat up and swung his legs over the side of the slab. He was stiff and covered with minor cuts and bruises, but nothing really serious as far as broken bones or deep contusions.

His back, on the other hand, was a different story. He could barely bend, either forward or backward.

For the first time, he scrutinized his cell. He guessed it was approximately seven feet by eight feet with a very high ceiling, maybe twelve or thirteen feet. The height only served to make the walls look even closer, more oppressive.

The concrete slabs with their menacing iron stocks could not have been more than eighteen to twenty inches wide and slightly sloped toward the end where the stocks were embedded in the cement. The narrow wood door with its boarded-up transom filled the width between the ends of the slabs. Walking space was limited to about twenty-four inches by eight feet. The cell reminded Jerry of a small closet.

But more depressing than its claustrophobic size was its soiled interior. Every surface was caked with dirt and grime from years of tortured bodies living in their own urine, excrement, blood, and sweat. There was a small, square drain hole in the middle of the wall at the floor, which Jerry later learned was connected to an open sewer where the camp's garbage and human waste were deposited. The air was putrid and stale smelling, with no hint of circulation.

Territorial spiders filled every corner, challenging flying cockroaches for ants and other crawling vermin in the tiny space. As Jerry studied these various insects, a rat the size of a small cat slimed out of nowhere, loped over to sniff the concrete slab in front of him, then scurried into a dark corner underneath.

About that time, he heard the sound of keys rattling in the lock. The door banged open, and a guard wearing a rumpled, light-green uniform and a pith helmet shoved in a tin plate holding a scant two cups of rice, a small jug of water with a tin cup, and a smelly bucket, Jerry's new toilet. The guard said nothing but turned and slammed the door shut behind him.

The new prisoner picked up his plate. The rice was full of

grains that were yellow-brown and segmented. He realized these were worms mixed in with the rice. He started to pick them out, but doing so would have greatly diminished what he had to eat, and he was really hungry. At least they were not moving; they were dead, they had been boiled, and they were protein. He held the plate in both hands.

God, at least I have something to eat. Thank you for this meal . . . even if it is filled with worms.

And without another thought, he consumed every grain. He was still hungry when he finished.

■　■　■

Later that same day as he sat in silence, from out of nowhere a voice called out, "Hey, new guy." At first, Jerry thought he was hearing things. He remained quiet. Then a few seconds later, it came again, "Hey, new guy . . ."

Jerry continued to hesitate. He was still adjusting, still trying to get his mind wrapped around the fact that he was captured—in prison—and he wasn't sure who this person was. Could the voice be trusted? He didn't answer.

There was silence for a moment, then it came again. "New guy. I'm Commander Bill Franke, F-4 pilot, shot down on 24 August—I'm a few cells down. Who are you?"

Suddenly, it became one of the most uplifting moments Jerry had ever experienced—now that he felt confident it was a bona fide military person—and just hearing the voice of another American was overwhelming.

"I'm Captain Tom Curtis, sir, shot down on 20 September, near Vinh—HH-43 pilot, during a rescue mission," said Jerry.

"All right, Captain. Are you okay?" responded Commander Franke.

"Yes, sir, I'm okay," Jerry said. He didn't bother to explain his back problems. Pilots assume if you've crashed, if you've been shot down, there's probably some kind of injuries. What Franke wanted to know was his general physical condition.

"You are in what we call Heartbreak Hotel." Commander Franke quickly explained that previous airmen had named this part of Hoa Lo Prison. Somebody evidently was an Elvis fan and remembered words from the number one hit recording, feeling so alone he could die.

"You make shoot-down number thirty, best I can figure," said Bill Franke. "And listen: we communicate with a tap code," he continued.

Jerry suddenly thought he heard someone outside in the corridor. He stooped down to look underneath the bottom of his cell door to see if anyone was there. It seemed to be clear—but lightning pain shot through his back, reminding him of his injury.

"It looks clear," said Jerry.

Franke continued to talk. "We use a five-by-five grid filled with a twenty-five-letter alphabet minus *K*. Just substitute *C* when you need to spell with a *K*. The top row across is *ABCDE*, second row across is *FGHIJ*, and so forth. There's a grid scraped into the walls in your cell somewhere—can you find it?"

"Hang on," said Jerry, and he began to look. The walls were gray, at one time whitewashed with some kind of stain but now covered in dirt and soot. At first glance, it looked like there were marks everywhere. Suddenly, toward the back of one corner, it appeared there might be something with letters. It was scratchy and unclear, but sure enough, when he scrutinized it closely, Jerry saw a tiny grid, five rows across and five rows down, the spaces filled in with the alphabet, minus *K*.

"I found it," Jerry said back.

Commander Franke explained this "tap" method of communicating could be rapped on the walls with knuckles or fists, elbows or cups . . . but it could also be coughed, sniffed, swept with broom strokes, slapped out with wet clothes, waved with hands. The letter B, for example, would be one tap, indicating the first row, then pause; next, two taps, indicating the second letter across.

He also gave Jerry a stern warning. "Communicating is risky business—if you're caught, you'll be punished." He elaborated no further.

Franke went on to tell Jerry that an earlier prisoner, Captain Carlyle S. "Smitty" Harris, had brought the "tap code" into the prison.

In later years, Jerry heard the entire, remarkable story. When Smitty memorized it in survival school, he had no idea what an incredible gift he would be giving hundreds of men in captivity.

Harris had been the fifth prisoner taken by the North Vietnamese after being shot down in his F-105 on April 4, 1965. During survival training, he had heard one of his instructors mention a type of code used in previous POW situations where Morse code was too lengthy or too complicated for easy communication.

After class, Harris asked his instructor more about it. It was then he learned the tap code, used by servicemen as early as World War I. As Commander Franke explained to Jerry, *C* is used in place of *K*, since *C* is used more frequently in spelling.

The letters *A*, *F*, *L*, *Q*, and *V* form the first letters of each row going down.

Later, Jerry also learned that just a few days before his confinement in cell #1 at Heartbreak Hotel, Colonel Robbie Risner, later Brigadier General Risner, had occupied the same cell. Risner, one of the senior officers imprisoned in Hanoi, would lead and inspire the hundreds of men who would be incarcerated over long years with his personal courage and commitment, as did several other senior-ranking officers.

Using a rusty nail, Risner had scratched into the cell wall this soul-saving grid. And, incidentally, on the same day Jerry was shot down, Risner had issued an order through the camp that all prisoners would be required to memorize and use the tap code.

For Jerry, it was an inexpressible gift to be able to communicate with other Americans, men dedicated to helping one another through all manner of suffering.

Suddenly, Commander Franke gave a loud cough, indicating a guard was nearby. All went silent.

But Jerry had been thrown a lifeline, and as a believer, he recognized the trace of God's divine hand. He thanked God for the gift of the tap code.

The tap code represented what would become one of the most precious resources the men who endured imprisonment in Vietnam possessed—communication. As God himself had once said, "It is not good for man to be alone."

PART 2

THE PRISON YEARS
1965–1973

CHAPTER 6
CHAIN OF COMMAND
SEPTEMBER–DECEMBER 1965

THE WINTER OF 1965 proved to be one of the coldest on record for the country of North Vietnam. Though there was no snow except up in certain mountain passes, the temperatures plunged—an unfortunate circumstance for those men within prison cells in Hanoi.

Initially the Vietnamese guards ignored their new captive in cell #1 at Heartbreak Hotel. Jerry began taking note of sounds around him, beginning with deep percussion notes reverberating from metal gongs struck decisively at dawn, or earlier. Then several times during the day, this was repeated to mark the hours, the changing of the guards, and other duties within the prison compound. Otherwise, oppressive silence permeated its dark interiors.

One day as he was attempting to determine how many days

he had been a POW—he guessed over three weeks—his cell door suddenly burst open. There stood two guards with rifles, using them to motion him forward. Since this was the first time he had been out of his cell after entering Hoa Lo, he had no idea their intentions. *What's this about?* he thought.

As he emerged through his door, they pointed across the narrow hall to the cell directly in front of his. He took the opportunity to glance at his surroundings.

Dimly lit masonry walls painted dark gray formed deep shadows all up and down the narrow passageway. This cramped corridor seemed to be lined with cells on either side. From what he could determine, each cell had heavy wood doors about two feet wide like his, with a "Judas opening," or peephole, about three-fourths of the way up. Jerry wondered how many other prisoners might be there. So far, he only knew of one, Commander Bill Franke, who had told him about the tap code.

When he stepped into the cell across the hall, the guards motioned him toward the back wall. There, a small showerhead mounted about halfway up spewed a narrow stream of water.

One guard motioned with his head, then said, "Go!" It was the first time any of the turnkeys had spoken any English to him. Usually it was "talkey-pointy," with motions and signs indicating what they wanted him to do.

Jerry wasted no time stripping off his filthy prison pajamas. He hadn't bathed since the beginning of his ordeal. And even though only a cold trickle limped out of the spigot, it was a welcome relief just to go through the motions of showering.

He stepped into the water, letting it fall on his shoulders and roll down onto his chest. He was so dirty, the rivulets scored the front of his body. He turned around, wet his back, then forward again. He lifted his face up into the water, stepped away, and shook his head.

At this point he opened his eyes looking upward. That's when he saw it: a message scrawled well above his head, so high a person would have had to be standing on someone else's shoulders to scratch it into the cement.

But he saw the words clearly—in English—a phrase Americans in the 1960s would have recognized immediately: "Smile, You're on Candid Camera." It was the signature line from Allen Funt's wildly popular television series that introduced the world to reality TV. When Jerry looked up and saw the scribbling, it filled him momentarily with absolute delight. A million miles from home, and yet a touch of Americana hanging over him. Few other short sentences could have buoyed his spirits more. He laughed out loud.

"Stop!" The guard motioned for him to put on his stained pajamas again. Then a few steps across the corridor, and he was back in cell #1, the door banging shut behind him, alone once more.

Jerry sat down on the concrete slab, still chuckling. The effects of that moment of hilarity carried him through the day. He knew it had to be the zany humor of an American located somewhere else within these prison walls.

Later that night, his prayers began as usual. He thought about his son and little daughter, Tommy and Lori, and wondered what Terry would tell them.

Give my family hope and strength. Give us all strength. Please let them know I'm alive.

Then he thought about his first shower again.

God, you knew I needed that today. I needed to laugh.

Jerry wondered who wrote those words on the wall and how they did it. It was so high up. He decided to make a point of finding out.

■ ■ ■

Solitary confinement stretched on—a monotonous dragging of time, minute by minute, hour by hour, day by day, without stimulus of any kind. There were no books, no television, no phone, no writing, no objects, no change of light or color, no variation of room or space, no visual contact with other human beings. Jerry wasn't sure if there were any other prisoners in this section of the prison. Mostly, he was alone with his thoughts.

The rules were printed and posted inside the cells: first and foremost, there was to be absolutely no attempt at communication between prisoners. No talking, whispering, taps, or sounds of any sort.

There were to be no attempts to peer into other cells—no peeking beneath doors or between window slats or through tiny holes bored in the walls. Punishment was promised, swift and brutal, for the least infraction. It appeared a man would need to be really motivated even to attempt communication.

Jerry found this to be painfully true one day after getting caught trying to whisper to Commander Franke. Jerry had not heard from him in a few days and wasn't sure what had happened to him. When he called out to him as loudly as he dared, two guards rushed into his cell.

One had a rifle and stood close by. The other motioned for him to get on the slab—he slapped his hand down several times, indicating for Jerry to lie down. Neither spoke any English.

As soon as Jerry sat, the guard pushed him to his back, then clamped one of the rusty stocks tightly around one ankle, securing it in place. After that, he backed out of the cell and slammed the door shut.

Now, with movement severely restricted, solitary confinement took on an even more oppressive quality. Adding to the lack of any stimulus, physical restriction produced unrelenting discomfort—the inability to relieve pressure on joints, since Jerry could execute only a bare minimum of change in body position.

Minutes and hours passed tediously, a gnawing progression of monotony that ate away at the mind without release. For many POWs, the mental torture of solitary confinement would prove to be their first and most difficult test.

Now that Jerry was in stocks, the days of being alone threatened to strangle him. He had to do something. He turned to God.

Lord, I feel I'm being sucked down. I need you. Help me with this . . .

Within these long moments, hours, and days, he had the time to think—and to think deeply—about himself, his life, his actions, his family, and his faith.

One of the first things Jerry did as he was in stocks on his concrete slab was to review his entire life, beginning with childhood as far back as he could remember. He thought through his earliest recollections of his parents, his eight siblings, and what he had learned and experienced through his growing-up years.

Since he was the youngest child, several older brothers and sisters were out in the world, employed, when he came along. The next to him in age was a sister, Mazine, two years older—they always had been close. He knew she would have taken the news about his being shot down so very hard. Not knowing what had happened to him would be difficult for all his brothers and sisters to cope with, but especially for her.

Mazine, he thought, *you still owe me four dollars.* He smiled, remembering his sixth birthday, when an older brother had given him five one-dollar bills, a lot of money for most anyone living in the rural areas of the United States in the thirties, but especially for a youngster.

On that evening, when Mazine had found out about her younger brother's monetary bonanza, she headed toward the pasture, walking quickly, her face contorted in deep thought. She knew Jerry was responsible each afternoon for herding the half-dozen or so cows back to the pen next to the house, one of many tasks relegated to the youngest member of the family. Even at six years old, he shouldered all the tasks with little complaining.

She formulated a plan, one that would rest on two traits Jerry seemed to have been born with—amiability and generosity. As she walked alongside him, she began her sad story with down-turned lips.

"You know, Jerry, I don't have any money." She looked over at her six-year-old sibling, swinging his arms, engrossed in moving the cows along. "And there's something in town I really want to buy."

As Jerry lay alone in his cell, he could see Mazine in the light of that Texas sunset as clearly as if the moment had happened yesterday. He could see her pouting face, could hear the cows shuffling along.

"If you were a good little brother, you would give me a dollar." She looked at him again.

After a few moments, Jerry relented. "Okay," he said, "here's a dollar." He reached into his pocket and handed it to her.

But big sister wasn't satisfied. She made her pitch again . . . then again. By the time they reached the house, she had four dollars, and Jerry was left with one.

He chuckled to himself just thinking about it. *Sis, when I come home, I'm going to get those four dollars you owe me.*

His large family always had been close. They loved each other, laughed together often, and seldom had cross words, except for Jerry's father, a cantankerous, outspoken man who had been on his own since he was thirteen years old. His difficult personality often led to outbursts of anger, and at times he was just plain hard to get along with.

Jerry recalled an incident one day as a young teenager when several family members stood around the kitchen table at their farm. His father had begun yelling about something, getting angrier by the minute. Jerry, fourteen years old, crept up behind him and pinned his father's arms to his sides in a bear hug.

His father broke loose and spun around, cussing at his youngest. Jerry stayed calm and just grinned. The other family members winked at each other with knowing looks. Later they said that was the day they realized Jerry was no longer a boy but a man.

Now in his prison cell, Jerry prayed for his father, who had refused to go to church all his life. His mother, the quiet spiritual leader of the family, had died four years earlier, so his father was alone.

God, I'm no longer there to talk to him about you. Open his heart so he will know who you are, and take care of him while I'm gone. I'm so thankful my mother doesn't have to know about my imprisonment.

Now, suddenly, his thoughts were consumed with his wife and family—what were they doing, what were they thinking. His mind stayed focused for hours and hours on his family. But his body was growing weary—such restricted movement produced incredible discomfort.

Fortunately, after Jerry had spent about four days in stocks, a turnkey came in and released him. At least he could use his toilet bucket—he understood now why the slab was sloped toward the end embedded with the iron stocks. And there even appeared to be a bonus: lying completely still for several days seemed to have helped his back injury, because he could move around with far less pain when he sat up.

But he continued to journey in his mind back through his life. At some point, he admitted to himself the experience was not altogether unpleasant. In fact, he could see where it could be useful as a means of self-awareness—to contemplate and examine one's actions, intentions, experiences, in total.

After Jerry reminisced about his earliest years on the farm, he concentrated on those times during his youth when his faith was developing. As a young boy, usually an older brother drove the family's buckboard pulled by horses, cutting through other farms to reach Crossroads Baptist Church, two miles away. Jerry's family lived in a tiny country community, literally at a crossroads—simple memories of another time and another place.

He thought about the Sundays that must certainly have had their effect on his young mind—the unadorned sermons in a country church; the old hymns with their gospel messages embedded in the lyrics.

Once after one of the services, an older brother, eight at the time, turned up missing, and they found him asleep behind the church piano after the service. Church in those days was serious and relaxed, all at the same time—and everybody knew each other.

Later, when Jerry was about ten years old, the family moved to the Houston area with a Houston address, though their farm was actually in a small country community. Their new church was Cloverleaf Baptist, meeting in a wooden structure that quickly became too small for the growing congregation.

For transportation to church, Jerry rode his horse, Son, a big, muscular steed his father had bought from an Army depot established after the Battle of San Jacinto, a key engagement in Texas history. The dark-chestnut horse probably had been used to pull supply wagons, but at this point, Son was eager and willing to carry his young mount to a little church, content to stay roped to a tree until Jerry returned to ride him home again.

Whether Jerry rode saddle or bareback depended on how early he woke up on Sunday morning. But even at this young age, Jerry went to church, whether anyone else in his family attended or not.

Jerry squirmed on the concrete slab in cell #1 of Heartbreak Hotel in North Vietnam, trying to find a comfortable spot. It reminded him of the wooden church pews back at Cloverleaf Baptist Church when he was a youngster, which sometimes seemed equally as uncomfortable.

Two of his brothers who attended Cloverleaf Baptist had both been deacons. Four sisters were also active within the congregation. Jerry began to attend Sunday school regularly, but he had one major hurdle to overcome—his deep-rooted shyness. He simply could not make himself get out of the pew and go to the front of the church, signaling that he had become a Christian, while everyone was watching, even though he felt a consistent inner prompting to do just that as early as eleven years old.

When he was twelve, he could no longer resist. After a sermon one morning, he got up and walked to the front of the church before everyone in attendance. His heart was pounding, and no one else came forward that day—he was the only one.

It was so quiet in his cell just now, alone in Hanoi, quiet like it had been on that Sunday morning as he left his pew. He remembered distinctly that momentous occasion and the sweet relief he felt when he publicly professed his need for Jesus Christ to be his Savior in a little country church located on the outskirts of Houston.

His commitment to the church flourished. When he was fourteen, the congregation voted to erect a brick building, keeping the older wooden structure for Sunday school classes. But volunteers were needed to complete the project. Jerry, along with many other teenagers, pitched in. They spent hours after school and on weekends hauling bricks from the brickyard to the new church site to supply building material for the project. Jerry thought back to the meals the preacher's wife had prepared for them—primarily shrimp and speckled trout, since their preacher loved to fish.

How I would love to have one of her meals right now . . .

His thoughts once more turned to Terry. When she came into his life, it helped seal his commitment to faith. After they were engaged and married, they worked together as a couple in churches wherever he was stationed. She continued to use her gifts of singing and playing the piano while he found classes to teach and ways to mentor youth. He had always loved teaching.

Lord, maybe I should have been a teacher instead of a pilot.

He smiled. After he joined the Air Force, he had been chosen to be an instructor in every airplane he trained in.

Now, however, reality had taken a completely unimagined turn, and being a prisoner of war was a different situation altogether. As Jerry lay locked in a cell in an enemy land, every commitment and every belief he had in an unseen God would be tested.

After several days, Jerry reached an end of thinking about his life. And so began the hard-core boredom of hours and hours without any stimulation. Solitary confinement required an enormous adjustment—he languished in his cell.

Since Jerry had grown up in such a large family with constant interaction, activity, and companionship, the loneliness crashed down upon him. With the mental cataloguing of his life completed, he suddenly realized that the sameness of day after day with nothing to do and no one to talk with produced a tedium so intense, it threatened to engulf him in complete internal panic.

Which is why when he began to feel his throat tightening after being in Heartbreak for about three weeks, the distraction actually offered a relief from the boredom. But the sore throat soon resulted in its own source of obsession—quickly becoming an issue of life and death.

Jerry had noticed it after he awoke one morning. His throat was slightly scratchy, just like the usual symptom at the start of a cold. But unlike the next step in the States, which was to go to a drugstore or to schedule a visit to the doctor, there was no option here in the damp, tiny cell. Jerry figured it was probably a combination of things—the stress of the past few weeks, the lack of good nutrition, and the increasingly cold nights with no covering except his thin pajamas. He hoped it would clear, but it didn't.

That night his throat was really sore, and the next morning, it was noticeably tightening. By the following evening, he could barely swallow, and by the third day, he knew he was in serious trouble. His throat had closed up to the point that when he tried to take in water it came out his nose. So he began to consider what he could use to perform a tracheotomy on himself, because he knew within a few short hours he would need to make this decision—or stop breathing.

God, please help me. Please help me . . . He repeated his pleas over and over.

Though guards acted as if they didn't really notice their prisoners' conditions, they actually kept a close eye on them, but not out of compassion. They knew full well what the poor sanitary conditions at Hoa Lo could produce: dysentery, typhus, skin diseases, and bacterial infections of all sorts. Normally, anyone suspected of even a slight fever—which might indicate typhus—was removed, never to be seen again. As the years wore on, this became more the norm than not.

But early on in the midsixties, with a relatively small prisoner population, the Communists were more intent on keeping each prisoner alive, if only just barely. In Jerry's case, his guard must have deduced this captive had a life-threatening throat infection, because on the third day the door banged open.

In walked a woman whom Jerry guessed to be in her

midforties. She wore a white lab coat and held one of the largest syringes he had ever seen—as large as what they had used for cows during his childhood on the farm. Without any words, she motioned for him to hold out his arm. The effects of whatever she injected him with couldn't be discerned immediately, but in about three days the sore throat subsided. This incident emphatically underscored Jerry's growing awareness of the absolute helplessness of his situation.

■ ■ ■

Just a few days afterward, in late October or early November 1965, the door of Jerry's cell unexpectedly opened once more, and the guards blindfolded him and cuffed his hands behind his back, then marched him to the rear of a truck. After a drive of about thirty minutes, North Vietnamese soldiers pulled him out and directed him to a new cell at a new location.

During the next few weeks, Jerry learned other prisoners had dubbed this camp the "Zoo." The section he was in became known as the Pigsty. Jerry's new room seemed enormous compared to what he had been living in. This cell was approximately fifteen feet by fifteen feet, yet the walls and floor, as in Heartbreak, remained the same—charcoal gray and filthy, covered by decades of caked dirt from neglect. Vermin, insects, and any number of crawling critters scurried across the blackened surfaces. In this space, there were no concrete slabs slightly raised above the filth. Sleeping was on the grimy cement floor with only a paper-thin bamboo mat separating him from its cold and varmint-infested surface.

In reality, the Zoo was located only a few miles from Hoa

Lo Prison, near the village of Cu Loc. This compound of deteriorating buildings possibly served several purposes in previous decades, ranging from a French film studio to some type of resort or recreation center. The grounds were littered with remnants of old posters, film canisters, and damaged reels. In the center of the compound was a fetid pool of stagnant water containing carp.

The general condition of disuse for the site could be observed most vividly in an old abandoned auditorium whose black interiors were completely overrun by varmints of all sorts and sizes. It was an empty, creepy place, pitch dark, with an overwhelming putrid smell. One isolated and completely sealed interior room off to the side was considered particularly onerous. Airless and totally black, it became the unfortunate place of isolation and torture for several POWs as tensions and brutality rose by late 1965.

On the first day of his arrival at the Pigsty, Jerry began adjusting to his new cell. He discovered quickly he was in a row of back-to-back cells with a thick, common wall down the middle. This meant there were three other prisoners sharing a wall with his cell, one on either side and one at the back. He also realized he was on the backside of the cellblock.

As he looked around, he noticed a tiny pinpoint of bright light close to the floor—the only ray of sunshine he had seen for several months now. Jerry crouched down and put his eye against the hole. It was too small to see much, so he looked around for something to enlarge the tiny opening. He found a small piece of metal and began chipping. He knew he couldn't make it too big lest guards discovered his handiwork, so he quickly gathered debris for a plug.

Once he had enlarged the hole slightly, he peeked through. Acres of swampy fields spread behind the prison, where Vietnamese women were bent over, harvesting what looked like greens growing in shallow water. As he watched, a younger girl waded into the water to help a woman he guessed was her mother. He thought of his own daughter, Lori, and wondered what she and her mother were doing together just then. Maybe Terry was teaching her to cook or play the piano.

He lay down on his flimsy mat thinking about his family and drifted to sleep. Suddenly, he saw Tommy and Lori drowning in deep, rushing torrents beside a road in Louisiana. They were submerged in a water bar, a large ditch-like structure meant to divert rainwater during heavy rainstorms. Often these culverts filled up quickly and could be extremely hazardous. He yelled to his children to hold on; he was on his way. He had jumped into the swirling current, struggling as hard as he could, holding his breath as he dived under the water trying to find them . . . He jerked awake from the nightmare, drenched in sweat.

Oh, God, be with my children. Take care of them until I return home.

These weeks since his capture had made him more reflective than at any other time in his life. But now, within this totally isolated and gloomy environment, he zeroed in on one specific aspect of his faith—his prayer life.

As he began to pray with a greater sense of urgency than ever before, he noticed most of his prayers were always more or less similar: framed the same way, focusing on the same issues, and really, using the same words. So he began to seek out the exact word that most clearly expressed his thought for each and every situation. He made the most concentrated effort he had ever made to express to God precisely what he meant.

After several days of this, he noticed he was right back to where he had started—with a more-or-less memorized prayer again, just with more precise words. When Jerry realized this, it frightened him. He made a commitment to pray as precisely as he could yet to pray exactly what was on his heart at any given moment. He committed to make prayer a genuine conversation as with a trusted, dear friend.

Whether it was because his isolation and loneliness were magnified in the Pigsty or because his discomfort was quickly increasing—the winter of 1965 in North Vietnam was the coldest of the century—Jerry's general sense of anguish seemed to be deepening.

There were no warm blankets or heat sources and only thin cotton pajamas to wear: he struggled with being cold soaked, especially at night on the cement floor. He hadn't had a bath now in several weeks, and the two scant meals a day were being reduced even more. He was hungry, tired, lonely—and it was Christmas.

As long as he could remember, this had been his favorite time of the year. He adored his family and looked forward to every part of the celebration surrounding the birth of Christ. He thought back to the eight Christmases he and Terry had enjoyed since they had been married, precious times full of activities, both at home and at church. And nothing pleased him more than to see his son and little daughter opening presents and getting up early to see what Santa had left under the tree.

His prayers on that first Christmas Eve in captivity began slowly at first. Jerry had always thanked God for the safety of his family back in the States. He knew Terry and the children would face difficulties but would be all right—they had a home and would be supported by a close family and many, many church friends.

God, on this Christmas Eve, thank you for your Son, who came to earth for us.

His mind rested on that thought for many minutes.

And, God . . . be with all of us now, in this prison. Keep us safe in these cold cells. Thank you that we at least have something to eat. Thank you for a free land to live in . . . As Jerry continued to pray, he asked God on this Christmas Eve to allow all the POWs to go home, to do whatever was necessary to bring the war to a conclusion. And as he prayed, he became more and more insistent.

God . . . this place is not where I want to be. I want to be with my family . . .

Jerry could sense his emotions welling up inside him.

I know you can do something, God. You are God! I know you can do something!

And then, suddenly overwhelmed with his situation, he began demanding, his inner voice now nearly screaming at God to change his circumstances.

Come on, God—do something! Get me out of this hellhole! Get me out of this mess! Do it now!

No sooner had Jerry prayed these words than he realized what he had done. Never in all his life had he crossed over such a line. It became crystal clear to him that his prayers, rather than petitioning God, had degenerated into demands. A deep silence fell upon him.

Immediately, Jerry knew the wrongness of what he had

been saying. Of course he knew he had every right to bring his requests before God. But he had no right whatsoever to *demand* anything of God. For God was God, and he was not.

This revelation was so profound that it took several minutes for Jerry to comprehend what was happening. Suddenly, he understood the authority of God in ways he had never understood it before. God does not just *have* authority—he *is* the Authority, the Author himself. Only God can make the final decision about the hows and whys of things—and God owes no explanation to anyone about anything . . . not even to a suffering believer in a prison cell in Vietnam.

This could have been a depressing revelation. But for Jerry, it was the most liberating thought that had ever entered his mind. Peace flooded every crevice of his mind and heart. A complete sense of trust came upon him, and he wept. He knew he might continue to face horrific situations, but God had been in control all along and would continue to be in control, no matter what Jerry's circumstances were. The Lord of hosts seemed to fill his entire cell that first Christmas Eve in captivity, and Jerry rested in the light of his presence.

CHAPTER 7

"WHY ME, LORD?"

EARLY SPRING 1966

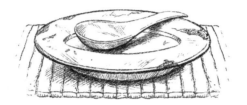

NOT LONG AFTER CHRISTMAS, Zoo guards moved Jerry to another cell. Instead of facing water fields dotted with floating baskets for harvesting, his new corner cell faced forward into the middle of the compound where a large, abandoned pool doubled as a garbage dump. Shuffling along, with hands tied behind his back, he saw carp sluggishly swimming in its foul-smelling depths.

Again, soot covered his cell, which appeared to be even more infested with crawlers, perhaps due to its closer proximity to the fetid pool. When he entered, however, he noticed a split-bamboo frame four inches high in one corner. A few days later, guards brought in two wooden sawhorses that raised the platform about two feet. It allowed him to recline without actually touching the frigid cement floor. In addition, he was given a thin cotton blanket, about eighteen inches wide and five or so feet long, but the cloth was a mere wink at warmth, nothing more.

Whether he was elevated or not, vermin explored his reclining body while he tried to sleep. He learned quickly that if he left even a morsel of food, rats would steal it. He was so hungry, he usually ate everything anyway. And he knew he was losing weight, even though he had been in prison only about five months. Diarrhea had set in almost as soon as he entered Hoa Lo Prison and was reoccurring regularly.

Despite Jerry's Christmas revelation, solitary confinement continued to challenge his ability to cope. When he awakened each morning, he faced hour upon hour of tedium: no variation of scene, sights, or sounds, just a dragging on of minutes, days, weeks, and months of being completely alone with nothing to do. He decided to map out a schedule for each day and began following it as much as he could.

The opening of cell doors marked time twice each twenty-four-hour cycle. Around 8:30 a.m., guards directed him outside to pick up a bowl of rice from the concrete walkway beneath a narrow overhang. At about 4:30 p.m., the same thing happened.

This chore of collecting food took approximately fifteen seconds start to finish, but it did provide an anchor both morning and late afternoon. Somehow these two small events helped Jerry organize his time. After eating the two cupfuls of rice, he would begin with prayer and then hymns, singing softly or just saying the lyrics. When he couldn't remember all the words to a song, he would make up words to fit. Then the serious business began: pacing.

Most days, he walked as many as six or seven hours. When he exhausted himself, he slept better, though still fitfully.

Back at his cell in Heartbreak Hotel, he had only about six feet, maybe seven feet, to walk, hit the wall, turn, and walk back again. For the present, here in a fifteen-foot-square room by himself at the Zoo, Jerry savored being able to walk nine paces in one direction and then back again.

Once every three weeks or so, guards led him to a five-minute shower with nonlathering lye soap. On one of these trips, a jailer handed him a small razor with a broken handle. Jerry hadn't shaved since his capture. The blade was so dull he suspected at least twenty other guys had tried to use it before him, but he managed to dry-scrape off a few layers of facial hair. It felt good just to do that.

While the turnkey led him back to his cell along a small sidewalk under a narrow overhang, he noticed dark skies overhead. The next thing he knew, a splash of raindrops blew across his face.

The sensation was startling. Since the beginning of his imprisonment several months before, he had been outside maybe a dozen times total and certainly not while it was raining. The cell door at this camp opened to the outside, so guards usually waited until precipitation subsided to perform their duties. On this occasion, the shower blew up quickly, catching them unawares.

Jerry was overcome with amazement at the astounding way fresh-falling rain feels. He leaned as far out from under the overhang into the spray as he could. It was the simplest of pleasures yet the grandest of sensations: he had missed it terribly, and suddenly he was filled with emotion.

During his prayer time that evening, he reflected on the day, his first shave, his shower, then the refreshing rain on his face. He pondered why he had never appreciated the marvelous magic of raindrops in times past. And he immediately knew why.

God, freedom forms the foundation of my life—I've never experienced being without it before—thank you, God, for allowing me to be born into freedom.

As the days crawled on, the thirty-three-year-old captain realized his successful communication with other prisoners would depend on his skill with the tap code. Because Commander Bill Franke at Heartbreak had been located a few cells away, it was difficult to tap loudly enough for communication to take place. They used it some, but when Franke could make sure there were no guards around, he would whisper loudly to Jerry. As a result, Jerry was still not speedy in using the tap code yet.

Here at the Zoo, however, he had recognized almost immediately there were probably other prisoners close by. He knew this because he could hear movement, sometimes coughing. However, when the POW on the other side of the wall tried to tap him a message, Jerry would forget the last letter while trying to determine the next. He knew he had to gain proficiency.

One day a banana came with his rice. It occurred to him the peel might be used to record letters. Searching around the floor of his cell, he found a small piece of bamboo. As the prisoner on the other side of the wall tapped out a message, Jerry would write down the letters. Whenever he received a banana, he hid part of the peel to practice, and he worked diligently to improve his ability to tap out first words, then short sentences.

The improvised banana peel primers increased Jerry's ability to pass and receive words quickly and accurately, a most opportune accomplishment because, unbeknownst to him, an event was about to happen that would challenge his skill to its fullest.

When Jerry awoke on the morning of February 22, a melancholy mood immediately engulfed him. It was his son's eighth birthday, and he had never missed any of his children's birthdays before. He knew Terry probably would give Tommy a party with friends and family, bake a cake, and watch him open presents. Jerry always loved these family celebrations.

The prisoner prayed, *God, I need to be home with my son. He needs a father. Why am I trapped in a cell a million miles from home? Lord, have I done something to deserve this—or . . . not done something I should have?*

In his thoughts, he pondered the age-old question nearly everyone asks who has ever faced a tragic event or deplorable situation beyond their control: *Why is this happening to me?* Jerry did not question God's authority as he had done on that first Christmas Eve in prison, but he did wonder why.

While he paced throughout the day, he mulled it over in his mind.

Is there some explanation, Lord? Why did this happen to me?

The questions seemed to rise almost of their own accord. But for the moment, Jerry sensed only silence from God. He went to sleep that night praying again for his wife and children.

A few days later, Jerry heard movement in front of his cell at the Pigsty. He quickly pulled up on the window ledge.

Steel bars filled these medium-square openings located about three or four feet from the floor. Large exterior wood shutters with slats fixed at a forty-five-degree angle restricted vision. When guards patrolled the perimeter, they could unlock the heavy shutters and swing them wide open, immediately monitoring everything inside the cell.

The prisoner, however, could not see out unless he was willing to risk being caught by guards. He could pull himself up by the bars and balance on the narrow ledge, then peer down the stationary slats. The higher up he could get, the farther along the concrete sidewalk he could see.

From his perch, Jerry glimpsed the legs of three people going past. Two were turnkeys, but the man between was obviously a POW. All Jerry could see of him was from midthigh down. His legs and knee joints were so horribly swollen, he could hardly walk. It looked like they placed him in the cell next to his.

Jerry surmised the man was a new shoot-down and had probably sustained these injuries during ejection from his fighter. Often from the force of ejection, a pilot's feet, once they come off the footrests, will flay in the wind blast. Sometimes parts of his body might even strike the canopy or sides of the airplane as the airman is propelled from his seat. No doubt this man then had been force-marched on injured legs from the place he was shot down to Hanoi. Jerry knew he was in bad shape.

After waiting a couple of days to make sure guards were not listening, Jerry took a chance. He knocked on the wall the "Shave and a Haircut" rhythm, which was familiar to Americans and used by the POWs as a safety precaution. Then he waited for the expected response of two taps, or "two bits." There was no sound. He tried tapping the first part of the seven-note couplet again. This time he heard two taps back.

Jerry pulled up on the window ledge and cautiously whispered through the window slats.

"Hey, new guy." Jerry used the same words that had been

a lifeline to him a few months earlier. "I'm Tom Curtis, helicopter pilot, shot down 20 September last year during a rescue attempt. Are you injured?" Jerry first wanted to determine his physical status.

The other prisoner identified himself and quickly explained his condition: "My knees hit coming out when I ejected—really banged them up. Didn't help walking on them to get here—took several days."

Jerry didn't know how much time he would have to whisper before guards got wise, so he went immediately to the tap code.

"Here's how we communicate through the walls. We use a tap code: simple alphabet grid, five by five: first five letters across top row, next five letters across second row, and so on. Omit the *K* and use *C* where you need to. For example, *B* would be one tap for the first row, then two taps for two across. Questions?"

No sooner had Jerry been able to explain it than he heard movement outside his cell. He jumped off the ledge and coughed loudly. Then he quickly stood up and began pacing. He knew guards would be watching them closely.

A few days later, as Jerry was sitting in his cell, he heard the "Shave and a Haircut" rhythm tapped on the adjoining wall. Jerry gave two quick raps back, indicating he was ready.

At first, there was silence. Then the faceless man on the other side of the wall slowly tapped out: *do u pray*. Out of all the questions someone in their situation might ask, the brevity and utter simplicity of this inquiry seemed overwhelming. Jerry sat a moment.

Here were two men who knew absolutely nothing about each other, not even what the other looked like. They had not had time to share much personal information—name and branch of service, what aircraft they had flown, a few bits and pieces of their history. What they did know was both had been stripped of everything: their freedom, their safety, their families, their careers. They had nothing.

The two men so far had not mentioned religion. Jerry had no idea the spiritual background of the man on the other side of the wall. And the man's question to Jerry wasn't about particularities like how, when, or what—just simply do you do this thing called praying.

Jerry tapped back *yes*.

A few more minutes went by. The man began tapping again: *did u pray before here*.

Jerry wondered what this prisoner with the badly injured legs might be working through mentally. He was suddenly thankful he could tap back a *yes* in hopes it would offer assurance, perhaps even comfort, to the man on the other side of the wall.

All was quiet for several more moments. Jerry prayed for the new POW he couldn't see. Then he heard the quiet knocking resume, although he never would have guessed the next question.

Slowly, the other pilot tapped, *what can u tell me about communion*.

In the utter despair of deep darkness surrounding both of them, it seemed the world itself suddenly hushed. Jerry quickly organized his thoughts and began tapping back simple, short phrases.

jesus died on cross for our sin . . . his body broken . . . we eat the bread . . . his blood shed . . . we drink the cup . . . to remember him.

The taps seemed like piercing rays of light transmitting the lifesaving message not even a detestable prison wall could stop.

Silently, Jerry prayed for his fellow prisoner but heard nothing more from him that night.

The next morning, Jerry wondered how the man next to him had fared through the evening. Sometime after guards made their rounds distributing the customary bowls of rice and small pitchers of water, Jerry heard several rapid taps on the wall. He sat down to listen.

saved water and little rice. will u help me with communion.

It seemed as if time stopped once more. Jerry answered, *yes.* He fetched a few drops of water of his own and a small morsel of leftover bread. Then he began a simple Communion service through the cell wall.

lord, forgive our sin . . . this is his body . . . take, eat.

Jerry ate his small piece of bread, knowing the prisoner on the other side of the wall was eating his grains of rice. He waited a moment, then began tapping again.

this is his blood . . . take, drink.

Jerry swallowed his water and waited again. Then Jerry tapped the last phrase from two defenseless men yielding to the highest authority there is in the universe.

we remember you jesus.

All was quiet. In the stillness, Jerry sensed once more a sudden awareness of God's glorious presence. It was as if the Lord were saying to him, *You ask why . . . and now you see.*

After this sacrament through the walls, Jerry began formulating several ideas surrounding his earlier question "Why me?" Throughout his adult life, he had believed the best way to lead was by example. To the best of his ability, he stayed true to his faith and the Code of Conduct he had pledged to his country as a member of the United States Air Force. But within the context of asking God to provide some answer to "Why me, Lord?" he knew the Communion experience answered his prayer.

Jerry always had recognized that one of his tasks while he was locked up was to pray for others in the prison. And this he did daily, sometimes all day. He took his praying seriously because he knew the power it had on men and circumstances and difficulties.

But the sacrament through the walls led Jerry to understand that wrapped up in any explanation as to why believers might experience horrific circumstances in their lives was *opportunity*—opportunity to fulfill a God-glorifying task, heightened by or as a direct result of the horrific event itself. The tragedy either brought others across a believer's path who needed to receive God's light *from* the believer or who needed to see God's light *through* the believer. Then, once engaged, that person perhaps would become a light bearer too.

Jerry realized he had been a conduit for God's glory to an unknown and unseen prisoner, and an eternal truth surfaced in his mind: the deeper the darkness, the more brilliant the light.

CHAPTER 8
BRIARPATCH HUMOR
SUMMER 1966

SHORTLY AFTER HE SHARED Communion through the wall with a fellow prisoner, guards transferred Jerry, trussed and blindfolded, to another camp around April 1, 1966. This facility, located thirty-five miles west of Hanoi near the town of Xom Ap Lo, rivaled the primitive circumstances of captives being held in the jungles of South Vietnam. It had no running water or electricity, and the food here was even less nutritious than at the Zoo, where a palm-sized loaf of French bread or a banana sometimes accompanied meals. So crude were these living conditions that POWs quickly dubbed the camp "Briarpatch."

After Jerry arrived, guards placed him in an area where small hut-type buildings replicated a tic-tac-toe grid. These seven-by-eight-foot enclosed cells each held a single prisoner in solitary confinement. Jerry occupied the cell located at the center of the grid. Cracks in the walls patched over with mud gave interior surfaces a cave-like appearance, and during summer months, tropical temperatures turned the huts into ovens. During winter, the opposite was true; cold clung to every surface.

Once the sun set, temperatures relaxed somewhat, but it quickly became evident that what created an uncomfortable situation during the day found its rival in an equally undesirable situation at night. Because of the camp's rural location, bugs came out in droves.

The first night, Jerry observed hordes of mosquitoes like a black blanket covering every inch of exposed skin surface. Fortunately, the next day, a guard brought him a mosquito net. He attached one end to the bars on the window and tucked it under his rice mat at the other end, holding it down with his feet. *How on earth could anybody survive out here without a net?* Jerry thought.

Right away he and the other POWs isolated around him realized a bonus unique to their new location. The iron bars embedded in the concrete caused reverberation through the walls. As a result, tapping communication could take place among all occupants. Though each was in a different cell, everybody could be "online" at one time.

These vibrations developed into a marvelous source for sharing information . . . and humor.

Here at Briarpatch, guards often were as irritable as prisoners. It was a miserable assignment for them due to its isolation and primitive conditions. As a result, they frequently gave even less attention to simple tasks.

After the first few days of imprisonment in this rural camp, Jerry noticed guards left his plate of rice for longer periods of time before allowing him to pick it up. One night, once he brought it inside his cell, he heard a distinctive rustling.

As he groped around the plate with his fingers, he discovered two large roaches—three- to four-inch flying palmetto bugs—competing for his supper. In addition there was a small rock or cement chip mixed in. He also thought he could detect a few grains of rice that were squishy and longer than expected. He guessed those might be white rice worms boiled during preparation. But he was so hungry, he fought off the roaches and swallowed the worms.

When he had finished eating, he tapped *gngb* on the wall, which meant "Good night, God bless." This was becoming the standard sign-off message between all POWs "through the walls" before going to sleep.

But then he decided to pass on his mealtime discoveries and tapped against the wall: *one roc . . . two roch . . . two worm.*

Almost immediately, he could hear the POW on the other side of the wall tapping back. Jerry pressed his ear against the surface.

beat u . . . two roch . . . four worm . . . one bug.

During successive nights as the POWs continued to count foreign objects in their food, every man within Jerry's grid of cells shared what they had found in their plate and the number. After a couple of nights, they simplified their messages by just tapping out the total number. One evening someone proposed whoever had the most would "win" and be proclaimed king for a day. Game on.

This contest continued for several nights, until one day the winner demanded a prize. After all, that was the least the others could do for him.

One POW tapped out: *u get dessert.*

Jerry rapped the walls with his knuckles: *ice cream.*

Another POW answered back: *whip cream.*

Next, someone added: *nuts.*

And so it went. Each night, someone was "crowned" king for a day, depending on how many foreign objects had been extracted from his food—or eaten as part of the meal. Then someone selected a delectable dessert to present to him, and each POW added a topping, a treat, or something to enhance the original selection.

In a very real way, this silly game actually lifted spirits at day's end. By mealtime, it was pitch black in the pens. The only sound was that of an occasional cough or shuffle or bugs flying. But if a captive had had the most foreign objects in his meager helping of rice, for a moment he had won a small victory, and the king for a day enjoyed an inspired culinary treat, if only in his dreams.

■　■　■

Jerry had not been in this rural camp long before he began to be interrogated. He had received a little information already through other POWs, who tapped out the letters *qz*, which stood for "quiz," the term POWs coined that encompassed any and all interrogations. Some of "the V"—a nickname the POWs used to designate their Vietnamese captors—spoke fair to good English; under these conditions, a prisoner exercised caution, restricting his answers to the shortest possible phrases. But often a guard might just be practicing his English. Always, however, the POWs were reminded they were the "blackest of criminals" and had committed many "war crimes" against the people of Vietnam. Often the lectures lasted for hours.

During one of his first quizzes, Jerry met an interrogator nicknamed Bug, who became more and more of a factor in the daily lives of men at Briarpatch. He already had a reputation for flying off the handle at the slightest provocation. Some POWs later described him as "an emotionally unstable interrogator whose wandering right eye, constantly jabbing index finger, and harping 'You have murder my mother' evoked alternately scorn and terror."

Bug had been lecturing for a long time, and Jerry sat still, listening. He suspected the interrogator simply might be practicing his English, because he remained fairly laid back and so far had shown no outward signs of losing his temper.

The questioner had been pressing his captive for a period of time about how US military rescue missions determined where a downed pilot was located. This sort of information could be useful to enemy troops on the ground. Bug was getting exasperated.

"How you know where to go when pilot go down?" said the interrogator, his voice rising.

Jerry realized he would need to give him something. From out of nowhere a bogus answer popped into the pilot's head. Quietly, keeping his face completely expressionless, Jerry asked, "Well, do you know what a carrier pigeon is?"

Because the V never liked to admit when they didn't know something, the interrogator said, "Yes." Perhaps with only his political vocabulary or his limited military words, he thought Jerry was speaking of a ship—most operations in the Gulf of Tonkin utilized aircraft carriers.

But he also might have been baiting his prisoner. Jerry couldn't be sure, and to continue down this path might land him in trouble. But he decided to chance it.

"You see, pilots have carrier pigeons with them. When they go down, they write their location on a piece of paper and wrap it around the bird's leg. Then the pilot releases him, the homing pigeon returns to base, and that's how we know where to look for him."

Jerry continued speaking steadily, with an impenetrable poker face, all the while staring the guard directly in his one stationary eye.

Bug listened and nodded. Fortunately, Jerry was never questioned about his answer, and he often remembered this conversation in heavier moments for levity.

Many POWs began developing their own signature sneeze or cough using expletives. These "sneezes" could be heard throughout the day or night, a little humorous reminder "that the family was all there, and things were normal; dismal as ever, but normal," said one POW.

After such cathartic moments, a POW might relate his successful ruse with additional satire. "I got away with murder" often followed the slightest triumph in the ongoing war of wills. Such minimal bits of mischief diverted attention, and even at times seemed like small victories.

Surprisingly, Jerry almost always knew what day it was while he was in North Vietnam. The POWs helped one another keep track. This, plus the routine of guards and the sound of gongs, served to help them with the calendar; the American prisoners knew when Sundays rolled around.

Back at Heartbreak Hotel and the Zoo, Jerry honored

Sunday by spending more time singing hymns and praying. Here at Briarpatch, with more contact with other prisoners, the men began having church "together" on Sunday mornings.

Early on Sabbaths, someone would tap on the wall *cc*, signaling church call. These taps would then be passed to as many cells as possible all over Briarpatch, and each man who wanted to participate would begin his silent service. Men also began having church call on Sundays in other camps, and those who wanted to participate did—and it was usually almost everyone. Men bowed their heads, prayed, and worshiped their Creator.

Since Sunday mornings had been important to Jerry his entire life, this became the most uplifting time of the week during his incarceration. There was something powerful—and comforting—knowing other POWs were near him, even if unseen, worshiping while he worshiped. Though he could not see, hear, or touch any of them, he knew they were having church.

The young captain began his silent service by "welcoming members" at his imaginary church door, something he had done many times at Horseshoe Drive Baptist Church in Alexandria, Louisiana. He thought of his many friends back home going to church—and he knew Terry attended there every Sunday with the children.

Terry always had been such a key component of their worshiping together. He thought about the small church they had nurtured together back in Germany with other military couples. They had discovered an old pipe organ in the building, which they cleaned and restored, providing Terry with a wonderful way to add music to their group get-togethers. He always included thoughts of her when he worshiped and pictured his children sitting with her.

Now, at his imaginary church service, he gave a call to worship, prayed, and sang hymns. Next he took up an offering in his mind, first yielding up his heart to God, then passing the offering plate. He preached a sermon by thinking of as many Bible verses as he could and meditating on what each of them meant. By the end of his church service, Jerry had been greeter, usher, choir member, and minister. Terry had led in music and singing.

One Sunday after completing his service, Jerry couldn't help laughing at himself. He realized how humorous it was to play all the roles involved in a church service—except of course for playing the piano and organ—when back in the States, so many people would think of excuses not to go to church. Even though he was alone in his service, he thanked God for the joy of church call.

. . .

Jerry was pacing one day in his cell at Briarpatch during the summer of 1966 and suddenly heard a commotion coming from several other cells around him. It sounded like doors swinging open and shut with many guards yelling and prisoners shuffling around. Then trucks could be heard cranking up and roaring away.

Later that same night, he heard commotion again, the sound of trucks returning and guards evidently unloading prisoners, doors to cells opening and banging shut. In the succeeding days, gradually and through much effort tapping on the walls, Jerry learned of the nearly unfathomable ordeal. It was an event that became known to the entire world as the Hanoi March.

Fifty-two American POWs were taken, primarily from Briarpatch and the Zoo, and provided "new" prison uniforms. The first thing American military servicemen noticed were the numerals stamped on the backs of shirts, usually three digits. The numbers were random, but the POWs quickly realized they represented much higher figures than had actually been shot down at that point in the war. This was their first clue the event was meant strictly for national public relations and for propaganda purposes—to make it seem many more Americans had been shot down than actually had been.

Guards then loaded the men on trucks and drove into the heart of downtown Hanoi. The parade began in late afternoon, but most men forced to march in it said crowds of people, in places ten deep, already lined the streets when they arrived. Later estimates set the numbers in attendance at over one hundred thousand.

As soon as the throngs saw the prisoners, people began screaming and chanting and grew frenzied with excitement. Many foreign journalists sympathetic to the North Vietnamese were on hand that night and recorded much of what happened.

Very quickly, rocks, bottles, bricks—whatever the spectators could find—turned into missiles. For the entire parade, prisoners walked with hands tied behind their backs, defenseless. Occasionally, the guards would stop and untie a few men at the front of the parade to keep appearances positive for picture taking. As emotions soared, people began darting in and out of the prisoners as they were marched slowly through the streets, punching and kicking the men who had been lined up two by two. Guards made no attempt to stop any attacks.

The men had walked approximately two miles, most now

cut and bleeding, some sustaining vicious kicks in the groin or blows to the face. Those who began to stagger were helped by other prisoners, who tried to walk next to them for support.

As they neared their destination, a large stadium primarily used for political rallies, hysterical crowds were near rioting. The guards at this point, recognizing their loss of control of the situation, quickly rushed prisoners onto the field inside the stadium. Panic ensued. The guards knew they would be held responsible if they lost prisoners in the melee.

Inside, bleachers filled quickly with screaming people, and over a loudspeaker a Vietnamese official continued to incite the mob with Communist propaganda. Guards actually encircled the POWs, realizing their only option at this point was to protect the prisoners.

Finally, the crowds began to calm and slowly exited the stadium. North Vietnamese guards narrowly escaped losing everyone they had forced into the Hanoi March.

It was past midnight before the pummeled prisoners were delivered back to their cells, most staggering and groping for any place to lie down. The senior ranking officer at Briarpatch later told the camp commandant that the Communists would regret this blatant disregard for the Geneva Conventions, and it did in fact have a negative impact on their image internationally once documentation appeared in newspapers throughout the world.

Jerry had not been among the ones paraded through the streets of Hanoi in July 1966. There may have been many reasons for this, but most likely it was because the Vietnamese had not allowed his name to be released as alive and captured. At the time of the Hanoi March, he had been in prison ten months;

the North Vietnamese would not verify his imprisonment for nearly a year and a half.

Even so, when the POWs returned to camp, he heard many stories firsthand of what had happened. And despite the incredibly horrific nature of the incident, Jerry realized humor had surfaced several times.

One of the POWs began to sing "I-I-I-I I Love a Parade" during the march, until guards silenced him with punches. One new shoot-down, who had just been brought into camp and thrown into the parade lineup at the last minute still wearing his flight suit, sustained several deep facial cuts trying to duck flying objects. Exhausted and disoriented, he innocently gasped to one of the men who had been a POW longer, "Do they do this often?" His question was later passed around prison cells through the walls, providing much wry laughter for seasoned captives—gallows humor at its cynical best.

Jerry could hardly believe all that had happened during the Hanoi March. As he learned more about it, he thanked God that the men survived. Many came away with injuries, but they all managed to survive.

Memories of his first shower at Heartbreak Hotel suddenly broke into his thoughts—those hilarious words: "Smile, You're on Candid Camera." He had not yet learned who had written it, but the message lifted him when he needed it at a dark moment during the unsettling first days of his captivity.

God . . . thank you for laughter.

He began thinking about what a precious gift it truly was—enjoyed by no other of God's creatures except humankind. For the POWs in North Vietnam, nearly all took comfort from any small moment of levity in an otherwise bleak environment. It helped lift spirits, lessen tensions, reduce loneliness. An amusing comment, however brief, redirected thoughts away from their misery.

One POW, Lee Ellis, told Jerry later how during the first three months of captivity he had been unable to laugh at anything. Then one day, after an offhand comment, it was as if the dam broke. He and his cellmate "fell into uncontrollable laughter, to the point of both tears and sweat. It was wonderful therapy that freed us at least briefly from the shackles of fear and worry."

As the summer of 1966 dragged forward at Briarpatch, Jerry would discover a greater level of distress than anything he had endured up to this point. He would need to call on every internal resource afforded him by his faith—pride, courage, and honor all would be put to the direst tests. The V were determined to conquer their captives, one by one, and they would spare nothing to attain their goals.

CHAPTER 9
BREAKING POINT
SUMMER 1966

WHEN THE UNITED STATES government removed the "2-S" provision of the military code, which exempted college students from the draft in late spring 1966, outrage spread on campuses across the nation. The action prompted hundreds of University of Wisconsin students to seize and occupy the newly completed A. W. Peterson Administrative Building in Madison on May 16. The peaceful protest lasted several days. Students filled the lobby area, which gave access to bathrooms, vending machines, and additional food brought in by sympathetic friends and family. The Peterson sit-in became the first of many protesting the war in Vietnam.

At the same time on the other side of the world, the V invented a form of "sit-in" all their own, using it with great effectiveness on their military prisoners to elicit information.

To fully understand and appreciate the war of wills that took place within Hanoi's prison walls requires at least a passing knowledge of two documents: the Geneva Conventions and the Code of Conduct. These official papers heavily influenced behavior and attitudes of both captor and captive in North Vietnam from 1965 to 1973.

The first, the Geneva Conventions, traces its roots to Swiss businessman Henry Dunant, who witnessed deplorable situations after the Battle of Solferino in 1859. His concern for the dead and wounded helped establish sweeping reforms in 1864 and also led to the birth of the International Red Cross. In 1901, Dunant became the first recipient of the Nobel Peace Prize.

Later conventions, in 1906 and 1929, addressed treatment of wounded and sick in armies at sea and treatment of prisoners of war. In the latter case, provisions stipulated humane treatment of all POWs. Subsequently, in 1949, a series of conferences upheld and expanded the three previous conventions and are referred to collectively as the Geneva Conventions. One hundred ninety-six countries are signatories, including the United States and Vietnam.

The second document, the Code of Conduct, played an even greater role for American military men who were taken as prisoners. Originally outlined by Colonel Franklin Brooke Nihart, USMC, and signed by President Dwight D. Eisenhower on August 17, 1955, the Code of Conduct contains six tenets to be followed by all members of the military. This set of policies governs behavior and attitudes, primarily as regards prisoner of war situations. Among these are what military members may reveal when captured: only their name, rank, service number, and date of birth. In addition, captured personnel will not give assistance of any kind to the enemy. The same stipulations are outlined in the Geneva Conventions.

For American military service personnel, both documents worked in tandem, providing a matrix to govern wartime activities. However, following these protocols required both captor and captive to adhere to the provisions within the agreements. As it became evident, interpretation of each varied greatly.

Besides these iconic documents, an unusual series of events led to a foundation of superior leadership, courage, and inspiration within the prison system of Hanoi, without which many POWs possibly would have succumbed to despair. A triumvirate of 05s, seasoned ranking officers, were shot down within just a few weeks of one another, very close to the start of the war and the taking of prisoners. These three senior-ranking officers, shortened to SROs within prison communications, defined much of the structure for survival in the eight-plus years of imprisonment. Their raw courage and faith in God and country kept POWs bound together as much as humanly possible.

These SROs were Navy Commander Jeremiah A. Denton Jr., shot down on July 18, 1965 (after release he was promoted to rear admiral and eventually elected US senator from Alabama); Navy Commander James Bond Stockdale, commander of a carrier wing, shot down on September 9, 1965 (later promoted to vice admiral); and Lieutenant Colonel James Robinson Risner, a Korean War ace, shot down on September 16, 1965, who was promoted to colonel shortly after his capture (after the war he was promoted to the rank of brigadier general).

As time went on, others entered into the prison system, including Air Force Colonel John Flynn, who was the SRO from the time he was shot down in 1967 until the POWs' release in 1973 (later he was promoted to lieutenant general). Flynn, however, was kept nearly completely isolated during captivity, which hindered him from being able to communicate fully as SRO. His courage in the face of prolonged punishment, however, inspired and motivated the entire prison population. Others stepped in to continue to lead as necessary, and through the years, many SROs in various camps continued what was established earlier by the three senior officers.

But in the beginning, even these committed, career servicemen had no idea what would transpire until the insanity of their new life began to unfold. As Risner himself, one of the staunchest of men, said later, when he first entered Hoa Lo, he had heard prisoners were being interrogated frequently and often experienced severe mistreatment during their capture and subsequent journey to Hanoi. He knew things were not rosy, but he "was still laboring under the misconceptions that we were going to be treated as prisoners of war." Once things settled down, he believed they would all begin to live a fairly predictable life as prisoners of war, lonely and spartan, yes, but within reason.

Within the year, the North Vietnamese had tortured all three of these men unmercifully, and all three had capitulated to one extent or another, along with dozens of their junior comrades. For those who were captured during the early years, the odds of holding out were long, even though these men represented some of the most courageous resisters. No matter how strong willed or brave, once the captors turned the screws, no one could last indefinitely. Though thresholds varied, they learned one thing: every man has a breaking point.

Spring and summer of 1966 witnessed the ramping up of

brutality across all prisoner of war camps in North Vietnam. No POW escaped the ferocity. The only question was how much pain a man would or could endure before submitting. Though it depended on the individual, later prisoner testimony recorded most of them seeing prostrate comrades, unable to walk, being delivered back into their cells.

After Commander Jeremiah Denton Jr., one of the senior ranking officers, had been beaten into compliance, he consented to film a message testifying to the "humane treatment" given to all POWs by the V. The powerful floodlights used in filming the interview with Japanese journalists on May 17, 1966, made him blink. He discerned an opportunity.

With his heart pounding and hands sweating, he slowly "blinked" out a message he hoped Americans back home would eventually see. As he gazed into the cameras, pretending to be overwhelmed by the lights, he blinked over and over in Morse code the letters "T-O-R-T-U-R-E." This was the first real confirmation of rumors that American prisoners of war were being subjected routinely to horrific bouts of sustained physical brutality. Later, when the Vietnamese realized what had happened, Denton, in his own words, "paid for it with blood."

After his return home, Admiral Denton would call the month of July 1966 perhaps the most torture-filled month of North Vietnam POW history.

One of the methods the V used to force many POWs, including Denton, into compliance with their demands involved sitting on low stools or small cement blocks. The punishment seemed innocuous at first; however, the severity depended on its duration. Guards monitored the prisoner, forcing him to sit without getting up, stretching, or lying down, and usually without food, perhaps without water as well: a North Vietnamese version of a sit-in.

During interrogations, everyone knew the less said the better. Each prisoner also knew to give as much misinformation as possible, especially when it concerned personal family details. One of the fears was that North Vietnamese sympathizers living in the States might seek out a family member for harassment, or worse. But the prisoners had to use extreme caution because if they were caught giving erroneous information, the V would double down on the physical abuse from which, over the years, several POWs did not survive.

The Briarpatch camp commandant, whom the Americans called Frenchy, constantly advised prisoners that handlers were particularly irritated with them and their attitudes. The POWs would need to comply and do exactly as they were told.

And here in this remote location, things could turn brutal quickly. "In terms of prolonged misery, no prisoners suffered more than the men confined at Briarpatch." POW treatment always seemed more vicious there than anywhere else among the numerous camps sprawled in and around Hanoi. Perhaps its isolated location caused guards, who needed no excuse, to feel even less restricted in handling prisoners.

In the summer of 1966, it became evident that a program of intense torture had begun. The purpose: to obtain complete biographies. The guards progressed methodically from cell to cell, removing men one at a time, and the V were determined to conquer their captives. How long they tortured the captive depended on how long he could last before capitulating to their demands.

■ ■ ■

Jerry's cell door at Briarpatch swung open with force. The guard, pointing his rifle toward him, motioned with the muzzle for him to stand up and come out. With a guard on each side, they shoved the prisoner to another small room not far away. When he entered, the interrogator called "Rat" sat behind the desk. Sometimes referred to as Louie the Rat, he was sneaky and shrewd. One moment he would be looking at his prisoner, then suddenly he would look from one side to another as if checking to see whether someone might be watching him.

The armed guards motioned for Jerry to sit on a small concrete block made from bricks. Cement covered the fifteen-inch-high seat and attached it to the floor. Jerry would come to know this room as a place of torture.

It all began subtly. Rat spoke, demanding Jerry write a complete biography. "Cuh!" he said. ("Curtis" was shortened to "Cuh." The V often used nicknames for their prisoners simply because their last names were difficult to pronounce.) "Cuh, you Yankee pirate. You war criminal! You come from United States . . . warmongers. You write and tell us all about your family. You give names and when born. You write everything."

Jerry sat, listening. He loved his large family—eight brothers and sisters, cousins by the score, his wife and precious children. This was something he told himself they could never make him do. "I will not write that," he said quietly.

Rat seemed nonplussed. "Yes, you will write, Cuh, you will do this. All about your family."

"I will not write." Jerry's voice remained steady.

Visibly twitching, Rat looked at his prisoner. "You not have help here. You alone. We punish you bad, Cuh. We try you for war crimes. You blackest of criminal." His voice elevated. "Do you want me to punish you?"

The minutes dragged. Something about Rat's questioning and demeanor this time was different from all the other hours of interrogations and indoctrination sessions. He seemed more intense somehow, less likely to be appeased.

Rat stared at Jerry. The prisoner slowly shook his head once more. "I will not write."

"Okay, Cuh. You leave me no choice. I punish you. You sit here on block until you write. You not get up, you not lie down, Cuh. Nothing on floor. We watch you."

Rat got up and exited the cell along with the guard. Jerry sat alone in silence to contemplate his situation. Since nothing quite like this had happened before, he wasn't sure what to expect. He supposed they meant for him to stay on the block until he relented—which he didn't plan to do.

After about three hours of perching on the low, cement stump, he thought how stupid it was to punish himself any longer. So he rolled off and lay down.

No sooner had he stretched out his body than he was jabbed full force in the back several times. He bolted up and looked toward the window located just a few feet away. There stood a guard wielding a long, heavy rod through the bars. Jerry jumped to one side, but the jailer prodded him over and over, landing blows anywhere he could—into his prisoner's stomach, legs, torso—all the while yelling, "Back! Back! Sit! Sit!"

The pokes were hard and swift. Jerry reluctantly sat back down while the guard gave one more stab for good measure, fortunately off the mark and hitting the floor. But Jerry felt the consequences of leaving the block—painful stinging sensations all over his body.

Day slipped into night. A guard brought a cup of water and a few spoonfuls of rice, but no mosquito net. After Jerry ate, he thought about his plight. *At least they're giving me some food.*

With darkness came plague: maddening mosquitoes by the thousands. He could hear them buzzing all around him and could feel them covering his arms, neck, face—anywhere they found exposed skin. He was thankful his hands weren't cuffed. At least he could swat a few of them away. Several times during the night, guards used flashlights to check on their victim.

Jerry continued to sit on the low, concrete seat. Every muscle and joint ached, and "bloodsuckers" continued their biting. At times, he managed to doze off for a few seconds. Once he actually fell over but quickly righted himself on the block, not wishing to experience the long pole again. Jerry's prayers remained simple.

God, be with me. Stay with me. Give me strength. I don't want to expose my family.

The night crawled by.

Finally, the next day dawned, and before long Rat entered the cell once more. "You write now, Cuh. You no have to sit anymore if you write."

Jerry took a deep breath. "I will not write," he said.

"You blackest of criminal! You sit! You no move. We not give you bucket to use. We punish you bad, Cuh. We catch you move, we punish." Rat left the room.

Guards brought Jerry a bite or two of rice and a swallow of water. Jerry felt fatigued; the rice stuck in the roof of his mouth. Guards reminded him again that he was being watched and not to move off the block. Jerry realized they were intent on a full-throttled program of unrelenting abuse.

About noon, diarrhea set in, something he battled from day one of his imprisonment. Like most of the POWs, intestinal problems were a constant: dysentery, diarrhea, bacteria, intestinal worms, and parasites. All these ailments evolved from appallingly unsanitary living conditions, poor diet, stress, and trauma. At least in cells, prisoners had pails. He now sat in his own putrid mess.

By afternoon of the second day, he couldn't hear anyone outside his window. Inside, temperatures soared, turning the torture chamber into an oven. He was exhausted. His back ached, his shoulders were stiff, his legs cramping. But nothing hurt like his buttocks—forced to remain crouched on a low seat placed extra weight on his hip joints. It felt like sitting on bare bone. He'd had it. He would take his chances.

Jerry had been standing only a few seconds when the long pole came lunging through the bars. Two guards jabbed as hard as they could. Jerry decided to see if he could get somewhere in the small pen where he couldn't be reached, but there was no such spot. In the corners, next to the wall, by the window—the room was tiny; there was simply no place to go.

With every vicious strike of the weapon, Jerry felt bruised. He wondered how much more of that he could take, especially in his intestines and groin.

The two handlers screamed at him. "Back! Back! Sit down! You sit!"

Finally, he realized it was no use. "I'm sitting, I'm sitting." Winded and with pulse racing, he collapsed back down on the block. At least he had been able to stand for a few minutes.

Nighttime came again, and along with it the insanity of gnawing insects. He had bites all over, some swollen to the size of a quarter. Now mosquitoes bore into previously bitten places.

Deep into the night, Jerry prayed with increasing intensity. Even now, he continued prayers of thanksgiving for his family. *Thank you, Lord, for keeping my family safe, for letting them live in a free country, for our church family . . .*

He knew their friends back home would be taking care of them, supporting them. God would see to that; he was confident. These thoughts brought comfort.

The words of Psalm 62, which had always been one of his favorites, floated in and out of his mind.

My rock . . . my strength . . . Lord, help me endure . . .

Protecting his brothers and sisters, cousins and other family members from possible harm kept his resolve going through the second night. Heavy exhaustion, however, began to set in.

The next morning guards gave him only a few sips of water. They withdrew food. Jerry knew it wouldn't take long now for generalized weakness to take hold. He prayed for strength.

By noon of the third day, he drifted in and out—not hallucinating exactly, but drifting. His body hurt all over, particularly his tailbone. Welts where mosquitoes had had their fill were now red and swollen. He had no control of either his bowels or his bladder; excrement and bloody urine drenched his pajamas, causing them to stick to his skin.

Still he sat, determined not to write a biography that might jeopardize his family.

On the third day—with no food, only a few sips of water, and loss of bodily fluids—total dehydration set in. Had he not been in so much pain, he would have collapsed. He tried shuffling his legs in as many different positions as he could. No adjustment brought relief. This was slow torture meant to bring submission.

Rat came into his cell just once on the third day and glared at him. Jerry shook his head no. The frustrated interrogator turned on his heel and went back out.

Somehow Jerry made it through the third night, now without water or food. His mouth was cotton dry; he could barely make a sound. Yet he remained unyielding.

The fourth morning, Rat entered the cell once more. He stood slightly away from Jerry, who was a complete mess—dazed, hunched over, and reeking of acrid odors.

"Cuh, you will write now. You will write!" Rat's face hardened, and his voice revealed the total exasperation brought on by this uncooperative prisoner. When Jerry slowly repeated his intention of not acquiescing, Rat looked as if he was going to lose it. Jerry thought he must be under pressure from higher-ups to elicit as many biographies as possible from the prisoners.

"You leave me no choice. I punish you, Cuh! You blackest of criminals!" Rat was fuming but did nothing. He left his prisoner to suffer through the day.

That night, however, Rat returned. He motioned the guards into the pen, who immediately set about to secure Jerry's hands behind his back with metal handcuffs. They then shoved him, bent over and limping, down a dirt alleyway between the buildings, out beyond the compound into an open field. When they reached a black pit about five feet deep dug into the earth with a sloping entrance, they stopped at its edge.

Here they bound Jerry's feet together and blindfolded him. After knocking him to the ground, they pushed him into the hole. The last thing Jerry heard Rat say was "You will write, Cuh!" The interrogator spun on his heels and walked away.

Jerry had been a prisoner of war now about ten months. He had been struck many times, butted with rifles, and clamped into stocks. He had battled loose bowels, dysentery, rashes, blisters, and near suffocation from a closed throat. He had experienced loneliness and hunger he never knew existed. But he had not been tortured. This time he knew guards had no intention of stopping until they achieved their goal.

Jerry's knees buckled when his bare feet hit the bottom of the pit. Straining upward, he raised his torso as much as his trussed hands and legs allowed. As soon as guards moved away from the edge, Jerry tried to nudge the blindfold off by rubbing his face against the ground and his shoulder.

He finally managed to peek out from under one edge. At the bottom of the pit on the left side, he saw an opening into a small space completely underground. Jerry surmised it was probably a bunker or foxhole, perhaps used for shelter during air raids. Another possibility floated across his mind—if he died here, all they would need to do would be to throw some dirt over his body.

By morning, his shoulders and arms throbbed incessantly. He bent forward, nose nearly touching his knees, trying to avoid sliding through the hole on the left. He didn't want to be completely underground.

Jerry felt miserable, but he continued to resist. Another reason POWs fought so hard to hold out was because of the next guy: if torturers were occupied with them, their fellow prisoners were still in their cells, relatively unharmed. Nearly every thought now was directed to God.

Strength . . . God . . . Give me strength . . . to keep going . . .
Oh, God . . .

Over and over he prayed for endurance.

The effects of dehydration and lack of food made Jerry light-headed and weak. One time he thought he heard someone cry out in the distance. He lay bound through the following morning and into the evening.

During his second night in the pit, mosquitoes once again covered his head and neck, though now, with hands bound, he had to endure their bites; he felt bugs crawling over his feet. By the next morning in the pit, he could breathe only through his mouth; his throat was so parched, he managed only partial swallows. His hands, badly swollen, bore marks where metal cuffs scraped away flesh.

A few weeks before, he had developed beriberi, a condition resulting from a lack of vitamin B, which, once established, lasts for life. For some POWs, the disease settled in their eyes, limiting peripheral vision; Jerry's settled in his feet, causing them to burn like hot coals continually. In this time of extended immobility, they felt distended and fiery.

As he entered the darkness of a third night in the pit, he couldn't think clearly, fitfully dozing, always with God's name on his lips but no longer able to articulate specific prayers. Exhaustion and pain had taken their toll. He maintained just enough of his faculties to know he was close to the edge mentally.

Then deep into the night, it happened. He felt a slight nudging on his upper back. Once again, several small pokes . . . then he felt the weight of something dropping across his shoulders.

During survival training, military attendees had been

schooled in what they might encounter in the fields and jungles of Southeast Asia. There was a wide assortment of dangerous creatures, but none as lethal as the banded krait, a relatively small snake whose venom was deadly within seconds.

Jerry lay perfectly still. Maybe it was a guard kicking a few clods of dirt onto his back or rolling a few pebbles to trick him. But Jerry felt panicky and helpless. Once more, he sensed pressure and thought he detected movement again, this time toward his neck . . .

Raising his head, he croaked out, "Bao Cao," the required signal for permission to speak to someone in authority. "Bao Cao!" he repeated. His tongue made clacking sounds as he tried to speak. Within moments, guards reached down and pulled him up from the pit. Whatever was on his back fell off. They cut the ropes from his ankles. Jerry barely could stand and stumbled his way between two guards to the interrogation room. They splashed him with water—he was caked from head to toe with dirt stuck by dried bodily fluids—and unlocked the metal cuffs. His hands and feet were swollen tight, wrists and ankles bloody raw. Then they brought him some water and a little rice.

At daybreak, Rat walked in with pencil and paper. The prisoner slumped over to write a biography.

Jerry purposefully dragged out the recording process as long as he could. He mixed names and juggled birthdays, trying in every way imaginable to provide some factual information but, he hoped, not enough to identify correctly anyone in his family.

As he sat and wrote, he also learned yet another thing: remorse after breaking under torture was nearly as excruciating as the torture itself. He felt like a complete failure. All POWs experienced deep regret when they succumbed, no matter how long or how much pain they had endured. The Code of Conduct was their "guiding star," as Admiral Stockdale would express later, but a man could uphold it just so far.

Once back in his cell, Jerry considered the great questions in Romans 8: "Who shall separate us from the love of Christ? Shall tribulation, or distress, or persecution, or famine, or nakedness, or peril, or sword?" Jerry had experienced, personally, all these things.

A thought suddenly jolted across his mind. The question is not, as he had typically heard it formulated, Does God give people more than they can bear? Each person has a different capacity for bearing. The real question is this: Is whatever we are bearing capable of bearing us *away* from Christ?

Jerry had been separated from nearly everything: in the humiliation of pain and fear and what it did to his flesh, he had been separated from any inkling of pride or ego; he had been separated from his sense of well-being, separated from a healthy body, separated from loved ones and family, and in a couple of instances nearly separated from his mental faculties.

Jerry learned in reality the truth from Romans 8: no thing and no one would ever be able to separate him from the love of Jesus Christ. Even at the bottom of the deepest pit on the blackest night, Jerry would reach a point beyond which no amount of torture could take him. When he could bear no more, his soul came to rest on something impenetrable, like a rock beneath him, like solid light.

CHAPTER 10

FACE TO FACE

FALL 1966

IT TOOK JERRY several days to gain strength back after the debilitating torture session. He mostly slept, getting up only to retrieve his two bowls of soup and to use his toilet bucket. He knew God had been with him through his ordeal. Even when he reached lucidity's edge, he still continued to sense his presence.

Not long afterward, his cell door suddenly banged open. Anxiety gripped him: a cumulative effect of ongoing abuse. Jerry was learning that in prison life, anything out of the ordinary was cause for concern. If keys rustled outside the door or someone walked stealthily, fear kicked in—there was no way to know what would happen next.

The turnkey motioned Jerry out and down the alleyway to another cell door. His legs were still weak; he felt light-headed.

Once the guard unlocked the cell door, he stood back, motioning Jerry inside.

To his amazement, there stood his six-foot-two stocky crew chief who had been with him at Nakhon Phanom and had flown with him during the shoot-down, Airman First Class Bill Robinson. Until the guard left the room, they only shook hands, but as soon as the cell door banged shut, Jerry gave Robbie a hearty slap on the back and received what could only be described as a bear hug from the big, friendly twenty-three-year-old.

"Robbie, man, it is great to see you! How are you? Where have they had you?" Jerry was overjoyed to be talking face-to-face with the first American he had seen in nearly a year—and someone from his own crew at that. Neither man could stop grinning, and both talked over each other for several minutes.

"I'm making it, sir, I guess," said Robbie. "I think I got hairline fractures in my kneecaps and maybe one in my neck when we crashed down through the trees and landed so hard. I've been with Neil Black as a cellmate some, and some in solitary. We weren't sure where the V had you."

Robbie's normally slow North Carolina drawl was quick and fast—he was thrilled to see his captain again. Jerry was thankful to hear Airman Third Class Black—the pararescue jumper who had been on their helicopter when it was shot down—was okay.

"What about Duane Martin—heard anything about him?" Jerry had heard nothing of his copilot who had run into the jungle away from the crash site.

"No, sir, not a word," said Robbie.

"And Will Forby, the pilot we were trying to rescue?" said Jerry.

Robbie didn't know any more than Jerry did about Will Forby. They were fairly confident he had been captured because they both thought they had seen him briefly as they all were loaded onto trucks in the jungle. But the guards had blindfolded them immediately and forbidden them to talk, sparing no blows with their rifles to the prisoners' heads to enforce the rules. Then as they traveled from village to village on the way to Hanoi during their capture, they were separated from each other.

They continued to talk, sharing whatever bits of information each one had about anybody else in captivity. Robbie saw his captain had not changed but continued to exude a quiet yet powerful self-confidence, just as he remembered him back at Nakhon Phanom. Then he asked the one question foremost in his mind: "How long do you think we will be here, sir?"

"I don't know, Robbie," said Jerry, "but hopefully not much longer." He mustered up all the optimism he could to answer the young airman, but he had begun to suspect this might not be the case.

They had to whisper these questions and answers, because as Robbie explained to Jerry, "Even if they give you a cellmate, they don't want you talkin'."

However, on this occasion, both men conversed all the rest of the day and all through the night. Several times after dark, guards came and banged at their window or cell door. "Shleep! Shleep!" Yet for the most part, the guards overlooked the whispering. Jerry suspected guards were allowing him this visit, especially with someone he knew, as a reward for writing his biography after his torture session—part of the conditioning of prisoners.

He didn't care. It was joyous to have conversation again, and Robbie, with his gregarious personality, was balm for his spirit.

As they continued to share and catch up, suddenly Robbie remembered something. "Oh, Capt'n Curtis . . ."

Before Robbie could finish, Jerry interrupted him. "Robbie, why don't you just call me Tom here in this cell. We are in the same boat for the time being."

"Okay, sir . . . okay, Tom." When Robbie grinned, his whole face lit up. "They let me send a letter home."

"You're kidding! Really? I have not been allowed to send one—I have no idea whether my family even knows if I'm dead or alive."

"Yessir—I wrote one, and I told Mom to say hello to Tommy and Lori and to your father-in-law, but I used his nickname. Hopefully when she shares the letter with intelligence sources, they'll catch the fact that we don't have any relatives or friends by those names. Then maybe Mom will call your wife, and your wife will know for sure it was legit. 'Course, there's no way to know if the V sent the letter in the first place, but at least I tried," said Robbie.

"Robbie, that's great! We will pray the letter got to your mother. I know she will call my wife and tell her those names were in the letter. At least then Terry will know I'm alive." It was the best news Jerry could have been given, and he hoped and prayed the letter had made it to its final destination.

Guards allowed Jerry to stay with Robbie about ten days, then put him back into solitary. It had been a joyous time; Jerry was so thankful. But now solitary confinement seemed more oppressive than ever before.

Jerry began to realize he would need additional coping

mechanisms if he was to survive a lengthy imprisonment—the poor food, unsanitary living conditions, and physical abuse were all taking a toll.

His strong confidence in God had entered prison with him, and he had been optimistic always, even as a child. He exuded what child psychologists often expect as the birth-order characteristics of the youngest: easygoing, confident, looking on the bright side of everything.

Or maybe his sunny disposition stemmed from a near-fatal accident that happened when he was just a toddler. An older brother, Robert, was chopping wood when Jerry quietly wandered up behind him. When Robert forcibly swung back the ax once more, its blade buried into Jerry's face, opening a huge gash in his cheek, missing his eye, nose, and mouth by millimeters.

Since they lived in the country and the injury required immediate attention, his mother doused the gaping wound with kerosene and applied a butterfly bandage. As quickly as possible, they rushed him to the doctor, who cleaned out the wound again and applied another bandage.

The resulting scar would mark his cheek for a lifetime. Perhaps his outlook of a half-full cup rather than a half-empty one was, in part, a product of this event. Surely, for someone to survive such a horrific fluke accident, with no harm other than a scar, must indicate living under the watchful eye of a guardian angel. But whatever produced his ever-present optimism, it marked his attitude even in prison. He never doubted he would go home someday.

Now, however, he experienced a fatigue like he had never experienced before, a fatigue of the soul. He strained to adjust to the realization the POWs might be in North Vietnam for a long and indeterminate length of time—that unknown years of imprisonment might stretch ahead. He knew for his own mental health he would need a strong antidote to combat so much misery. Trusting his usual method for handling any crisis situation, he turned to God.

God, I am so lonely . . . Help me endure this. I miss my family. If I am in for the long haul, I will need your strength. You are my rock. Help me find a way.

And God, gracious as ever, began to show him a way.

. . .

A few weeks after Jerry's time with his former crew chief, Bill Robinson, he was pacing back and forth as he did every day. He had begun all the same methods of trying to pass time in solitary by walking several hours, praying, and singing hymns. He pushed himself even though the beriberi in his feet burned as if he were walking barefoot on hot coals.

Suddenly, he heard the distinct rustling of keys turning in the cell lock. He stopped dead still. He turned toward the door. There stood a POW, about five foot nine with a shock of thick wavy hair, now longer than he would have ever worn it under normal military circumstances. Unshaven and dirty, he looked like a vagabond, clutching his mat, thin blanket, tin cup, and mosquito net.

The two looked at each other for a moment. After the guard left, the POW held out his hand and said, "I'm Will Forby— shot down on 20 September last year. And I think you are . . ."

"Yes! Will! I thought I recognized you." Jerry was elated to see the pilot standing before him. "I'm Tom Curtis, the one who came to rescue you. Man, I sure wish we had been able to complete that mission!" The two men shook hands, united in misfortune by the same horrific circumstances. "How are you? Are you okay?" Jerry asked.

"I've been in solitary since I've been here. They've moved me a couple of times, always blindfolded. How about you?" said Will.

"The same. Took a round of torture when they wanted a biography," replied Jerry.

"Yeah, I know about that, too," returned Will, who told him about his months in solitary and then the torture he had endured also.

"What happened when you were shot down?" Jerry asked.

"I was flying out of Takhli, Thailand, and had just bombed a bridge. I was pulling out when I took a hit in the belly of the plane. My F-105 caught fire immediately. I was nose up and doing about 350 knots when I ejected. The wind blast really hurt my legs—caused them to flail around pretty good. As I was coming down, I actually looked over and saw my plane crash."

"No kidding," said Jerry.

"Yes, and then the wind took me into that wooded hillside, and I hit hard. When I tried to stand up, I felt gimpy. I heard Vietnamese militia yelling all around me, so I found a place to hide and stayed there until I heard your chopper about an hour later," Will continued.

It was the first time Jerry had heard the complete story of Will's shoot-down. "We had you in the hoist," said Jerry.

"Yes—I already was on. Then your helicopter was shot, and when I looked up, I saw you coming down right above me!"

"I know," said Jerry. "I kept praying, 'Lord, don't let me kill this guy by crashing on top of him.' I was afraid I was going to squash you like a bug! I can't tell you what a relief it was to discover you were okay!"

They both laughed, and Will continued. "When you guys took off down that steep ravine to get away from the crash site, I didn't think my legs would make it down, so I went back to my original hiding place. But they found me fairly quickly. They must have been militia because they seemed as scared of me as I was of getting caught by them. One of them started waving his rifle around and it went off—the bullet ricocheted off something and hit me in the forearm."

The two pilots exchanged the bits and pieces of information they had about their situation and what little they had learned about other POWs through the walls. As when Jerry had been with Bill Robinson, the overriding question surfaced. "How much longer do you think we're going to be here?" asked Will.

"I have no idea . . . no idea. Maybe not much longer" was Jerry's stab at optimism.

As the weeks continued, the guards allowed the two men to remain in the same cell. Since the V had as much difficulty pronouncing Will's last name as Jerry's, they had started calling him "Fo," short for "Forby."

During their conversations, Jerry and Will shared their backgrounds and, in the process, learned something of tremendous importance. It began with a simple question. Will asked, "Are you a member of a church back home?"

As they talked, they discovered the other's heart: "I'm a believer—God is my rock, Jesus my Lord," said Jerry.

Will Forby shared that he, too, was a believer. They both agreed that it was the one thing that had helped them survive the ordeal thus far and that it was an incredible blessing for each to know they had a cellmate who shared the same hope.

One morning after guards had delivered the morning bowl of soup, Jerry felt his lips cracking in several places. Dehydration shaped his existence due to recurring diarrhea and dysentery. Guards gave each prisoner a small, earthen jug that held perhaps a quart of water—he had noticed Will never drank more than half his allotment.

"You don't drink all of your water?" Jerry asked Will one morning.

"I've never drunk much water," replied Will.

"Man, you must be like a camel," said Jerry. Will grinned and passed his jug to Jerry, who thanked him. "This is a lifesaver."

Having Will to talk to was an incredible gift. He was a quiet person, amiable and easygoing like Jerry. They immediately became friends.

But they also made efforts to stay in touch with other prisoners around them. If they heard the familiar "Shave and a Haircut" tap, both would respond, one on one wall, the other on the opposite wall. Sometimes it was hard to determine where the taps were coming from, so each POW would begin tapping.

A few weeks later they had just gotten "on the wall" to communicate when a guard burst in. He immediately was joined by another armed soldier.

"You tap, you tap!" He was furious. He ordered both of them to lie down.

"Put hands behind back! Now, now!" While one held a rifle on them, the other stooped over and forced their hands behind their backs, locking them tightly with metal cuffs.

After the guards left their cell, they each rolled over and sat up, still on the floor. "Well, here we are," said Jerry.

Will sat silently for a moment. Now instead of wondering how long they would be in prison, there was a more immediate question on his mind. "How long do you think they are going to keep us cuffed like this?"

Later in the day when the guards brought their bowls of thin soup, they unlocked their metal handcuffs. But as soon as they ate, turnkeys immediately rushed back into the cell and cuffed them again.

The first night trying to sleep on the cement with hands secured behind their backs, Jerry could hear Will tossing around, trying to reposition himself. Jerry struggled with the same thing—there was no place that allowed much comfort for any length of time. If he was on his back, the weight of his body on his arms and cuffed hands beneath him caused swelling and numbness. If, however, he rolled over on his chest, eventually his shoulders cramped because of the angle of his arms pulled behind. Partially on his side or partially sitting up were options offering a little relief but only momentarily.

The next morning the guards came in and unlocked their cuffs. "Eat! Eat!" barked the turnkey, then turned and left.

Jerry rubbed his wrists. He squeezed his fingers open and shut trying to get some circulation back. It felt so good to bring his arms back around to the front of his body. He rubbed his shoulders for a few seconds, then gulped down the rice. After about ten minutes, the guards rushed back in. "Down, down!" one of them said.

"Wait! Why again?" asked Jerry.

"You tap!" the guard said. "We punish you." Both men now

found themselves in the cuffs, arms and hands pulled behind their backs once more.

Despite the vocal objections of both POWs, this form of punishment continued. The two cellmates began to feel complete exhaustion. Their wrists were raw and their shoulders and arms lifeless. Each protested when the guards came in. Jerry and Will tried to extend mealtime, the only time their hands were not cuffed, as long as they could. But guards were quick to show that if they tarried, their food simply would be removed.

This had been going on for a few days, when one night Jerry was startled awake. There was somebody standing next to him in the darkness.

"Hey, look at this." Jerry recognized his cellmate's whisper. There stood Will with his hands still cuffed but now in front of him.

Jerry's arms were short and his hips wide, making it impossible to do anything but remain in an uncomfortable position all day and night long. But Will had long arms and a small backside. So frustrated with their plight, he had begun trying to work his hands and arms down behind his back, then lowering them behind his legs until he could bring them beneath his feet and up in front of him. They both began searching for a piece of wire or any object they might find in the small piles of rubble scattered across the floor that could be used to pry open the lock.

At last they scrounged up a small nail, and after many minutes of concentrated effort, working it back and forth inside the rusty lock, Will sprang open his metal handcuffs. Then Jerry turned around and Will worked one side of Jerry's to free his hands as well. It was such a relief to have arms and hands released.

"You know we are in for it if they catch us," said Jerry. Will nodded in agreement. They knew they would both be punished severely if guards discovered what they had done, and because periodic checks occurred throughout the night, they were never able to sleep soundly, even though they were more comfortable. To prevent getting caught, they would keep one side of the cuff locked, but the perils were obvious because they would both have to try to recuff themselves before guards noticed they were loose.

The choice was agonizing: to have a respite from the aching discomfort or to risk a severe beating. They usually decided to sleep with one cuff unlocked and one eye open.

The guards kept Will and Jerry in this grossly restricted position for over two months. Jerry knew he would have had a difficult time undergoing such an ordeal alone in solitary. This, plus Christmas drawing near, his second in captivity, made him especially thankful to have a cellmate.

When Christmas Eve arrived, Will and Jerry shared stories of favorite traditions from their past. Jerry told Will about the large family he was from and how much fun they always had during the holidays. Will was from a smaller family, but Christmas was a very important time for them, too. They went to church on Christmas Eve for pageants and lighting candles.

They both sorely missed all the festivities. They went quiet for a long while, lost in their own thoughts of home. It was miserably cold and damp in the cell. Jerry would have given anything to be home with Terry and his children, opening packages and drinking hot chocolate.

Suddenly, noisy scratches on the camp loudspeakers broke through the oppressive silence. Then, the unexpected sound of an American's voice called over the speaker. The cellmates looked at each other, puzzled, then listened intently.

"Just wanted to wish all of you a merry Christmas and to give you something."

With that introduction, the beautiful baritone voice began. "O Holy Night" rang out through the entire camp, soft and clear as a bell. How that POW had convinced the guards to let him sing over the loudspeakers was a mystery, but it sounded like the voice of an angel.

Jerry had never heard the song before that night. When the singer reached the melody's crescendo with words imploring listeners to fall on their knees and hear the heavenly choirs, he was overcome with emotion. The simple yet powerful lyrics stirred him to the very core of his being.

Long after the singing stopped, the music seemed to linger in the darkness. It was a touch of the divine at the most unexpected moment in the most unlikely of places.

CHAPTER 11
·THE MIDDLE YEARS

1967–1969

MOST POWS CALL THE YEARS of imprisonment stretching from 1967 until the end of 1969 the "middle years." After a brief reprieve from harsh physical treatment during early spring of 1967, camps witnessed a ramping up of torture and interrogations and a general slide downward of food, medical treatment, and hygiene. Subsistence rested on the barest minimums; the middle years were nothing short of savage.

Military historians Stuart Rochester and Frederick Kiley record a cataclysm of abuses during this time that pushed nearly everyone in North Vietnam prisons to the edge of despair: "Almost all of the captives who were subjected to the crucible of the middle years experienced depression, nightmares, and a crisis of the spirit at some juncture." Commander James Stockdale termed the period "the melting experience," saying later that everyone tried to gain control of themselves in some way or another, to conquer one day at a time.

One factor loomed above the others, casting a long shadow of uncertainty over their tormented landscape: the gnawing possibility of growing old in these dungeons, or worse yet, never going home at all. It festered in the back of everyone's mind, breeding terror. The younger men saw many of their best years slipping away. Those with medical issues weren't healing. Men who had been there since 1965, as Jerry had been, began to acknowledge this might be a longer experience than they had imagined at first. Many wondered how they could cling to the cliff's edge indefinitely.

During the middle years, guards moved Jerry multiple times—four relocations in 1967 alone. He began the year at Briarpatch. Then around February, armed guards trucked him and Will, also blindfolded, the thirty or so miles back to downtown Hanoi into a section of the Hanoi Hilton nicknamed "Vegas."

Jerry's first stay here was short, and in June 1967, he was blindfolded, loaded into a truck again, and transported to a suburb in northern Hanoi to a place called the "Power Plant," also nicknamed "Dirty Bird." Here he stayed through the summer, and then in August he was moved to a nearby cellblock dubbed the "School." Later in October, guards moved him back to Vegas.

These multiple moves represented attempts to disrupt communication, keep morale low, and sometimes to separate those POWs considered hard-core resisters for additional punishment. Moving kept a prisoner in a constant state of flux. And after a short lull from abuse in early 1967, the beginning of the middle years also saw a return of all the old familiar ways the V administered vicious terror. Everything seemed to be collapsing.

. . .

When guards had come into Jerry's cell at Vegas, they told him to roll up his mat and his eighteen-inch-wide cotton blanket and to pick up the sweater he'd been given and his tin cup. Then, to his surprise, they told Will Forby to do the same thing.

Both prisoners were taken to cells at a place POWs dubbed the Power Plant. It was comprised of makeshift cellblocks within a larger, still-active facility known as the Yen Phu Thermal Power Plant in northern Hanoi, near the government district. The huge plant covered more than five city blocks with various supporting buildings including shops, warehouses, an assembly plant, and other smaller facilities. POWs nicknamed another area of the thermal plant the "School" since they found stacks of what looked like old Chinese textbooks within the cells.

Here Jerry experienced what living was like covered in coal dust. Black particles filled the air. Dingy charcoal-gray was the only color that could be seen, no matter where anyone looked.

The time Jerry spent at the Power Plant yielded good news and bad news. The good news was that during the day, he and Will were allowed outside for a few hours each day in an area near a temporary kitchen that guards used for cooking meals. The outside area was littered with debris and refuse, and large rats and other varmints inhabited these deserted portions of the huge complex.

But prisoners welcomed any reprieve from their makeshift cells because all windows had been bricked up completely. There was no air circulation at all, not even a wisp—each cell was like a tightly closed storage unit that sat in full sun. Summer temperatures rose mercilessly, converting these confinement spaces into suffocating ovens. Even with the added time outside, severe heat rash soon covered Jerry's entire body.

However, since the POWs were outside within a complex built for purposes other than use as a prison, the guards' anxiety increased concerning security. To lessen the likelihood of escape attempts, jailers shackled prisoners to one another with ankle manacles.

Here is where the bad news for Jerry unfolded. His ankles were too big for the metal ankle cuffs, so guards fastened one of his wrists to Will Forby's ankle. For over a month, Jerry and Will spent each day shackled to each other in this manner. Their only option was to sit on the ground for the length of their time outdoors.

Though Jerry could see other rooms being used as cells and estimated there may have been a dozen or so prisoners there, he never saw any of them. He concluded, however, that the prison population must be increasing substantially—which meant more and more US servicemen shot down—for the North Vietnamese to resort to using these makeshift facilities.

Yet there might have been another explanation: because the thermal power plant had been a target area for US bombing raids, Vietnamese authorities may have thought housing POWs there would deter further assaults, especially if US authorities knew about it. Jerry and Will had already seen the roof to their cell actually lift upward, as if in slow motion, from concussions during a bombing raid.

So to make the presence of these prisoners known, the V

would press the POWs into service to walk under armed guard to the main thermal plant in open view. Here they retrieved boiled drinking water for the prison cellblock. By this time, Jerry was suffering from severe dehydration, rashes, and blisters due to the extreme heat within his bricked-up cell.

On one of these occasions, Jerry experienced a small pleasure he had missed for a long time. After a guard unlatched his cuffs, he motioned for him and another POW to follow. Together, the two prisoners were given a chogee pole with a bucket swinging from the middle. These were normally carried across the shoulders by a single Vietnamese with a bucket on each end.

Under armed guards, the POWs walked through the streets to the thermal plant a few blocks away. Along the roadside, Vietnamese civilians would stop whatever they were doing to stare at the ragged-looking men. Their reactions represented extremes. Some people smiled broadly and even waved as they walked past; others picked up any rock they could find and threw it at them.

Once they got to the plant, a worker filled their deep bucket with boiled water, an item Jerry was thankful for. *At least we aren't forced to drink water that isn't potable*, he thought. After the worker finished filling the container, he took a pick and chipped away a couple of pieces of ice from a large block sitting beside him on a pushcart. Then he handed a small chunk to the prisoner.

Jerry put the piece of ice in his mouth—a cold, tasty treat that felt so good to his parched lips and throat. Since prisoners were never given ice, it was the only piece he enjoyed for nearly eight years.

That night back in his cell, as he lay prostrate on his thin mat on the concrete floor, he could feel sweat running down his face and sides. Though night had fallen, the air remained suffocating. His heat rash had spread under his arms, across his back and chest, and all over his legs, alternately stinging and itching from perspiration, especially in the folds and crevices of his body.

He had spent the afternoon making coal balls. These were formed from a mixture of coal dust and a little water and dirt and rolled into a sphere about the size of a baseball. Guards burned them to cook the prison meals, so Jerry never minded the task since it directly contributed to POW welfare. Once finished, he would stack them like cannonballs.

But the chore always left his hands filthy with no way to wash. He tried to keep from scratching heat rash blisters, afraid of infection.

As he sweat in the darkness, suddenly he thought he heard music. He strained to hear. *What on earth?* No, he wasn't mistaken—it was Louis Armstrong playing his trumpet and singing. Then he heard two guards walking and talking on their patrol outside his cell.

They must have a transistor radio with them, thought Jerry. The music stopped and he heard one of the guards say, "Satch-Mooo!" Jerry cackled. *Now that's funny—they certainly know good music*, he thought.

He was still smiling when he began talking to God about his day and the chore of fetching water to bring back for the POWs. *I never thought I could be so delighted over a chip of ice.*

As he mused about the incident, he sensed God nudging him to examine past events in prison for any unusual moment for which he could be thankful. The middle years were especially tough, but even now, Jerry found several things to be thankful for.

Jerry thought about his goofy-looking sandals cut out of rubber tires, the tread still showing clearly. They had been thrown into his cell one day at the Zoo. He smiled to himself in the darkness.

They are about three sizes too small, Lord, but they do keep my feet—at least the front part of my feet—off the cold, cement floor. He had to walk like a toddler when he had them on, up on his toes. *But I thank you for these rubber shoes.*

He still had them—they were sitting beside his mat even now.

Not long after guards had given him his sandals, he received another item he had come to treasure—a thin, blue cotton sweater. It was coarsely woven of dark blue cotton threads, similar to a mock turtleneck. Though the sweater was not quite as good as a jacket, it represented more defense from shivering than he'd had since he was captured. In summer, the sweater could be rolled up at night to form a small pillow, something he sorely missed in captivity.

So between the thin additional layer of clothing in winter and the makeshift pillow in summer, he called the sweater "my best buddy." He had expressed sincere appreciation to the Lord for his new article of clothing the night he received it and thanked God again on this night. It was rolled beneath his head as he prayed.

Just then he heard Will cough in the blackness on the other side of the cell.

And, Lord, thank you again for this cellmate. Thank you for all the things, even here in prison, you have given me to be thankful for.

Jerry began to understand that thankfulness, at times, must be intentional, especially in seasons of darkness. It comes from purposefully searching for the treasures of life: sometimes they may be the simplest things, like a piece of ice or a thin sweater, but God had placed them there for him to discover, to acknowledge, to find pleasure in, and to derive hope from—even in the midst of despondency. The intentional act of staying thankful, no matter the circumstances, anchors the soul while opening a door for blessings.

Jerry suddenly remembered a verse he had memorized in Sunday school as a youth, 1 Thessalonians 5:18: "In every thing give thanks: for this is the will of God in Christ Jesus concerning you."

Here in prison, God was showing Jerry how to *live* this verse, even while facing grueling circumstances. He was rescuing the rescue helicopter pilot with gratitude.

CHAPTER 12

TIES THAT BIND

FALL 1967–1968

IN THE LATE SIXTIES, Billy Graham held a ten-day crusade in Kansas City. Crowds totaling over 364,000 came from all over the Midwest by plane, train, and car and packed the Municipal Stadium. During a three-day youth event conducted at the same time, the arena filled to near capacity with people under twenty-five. Over ten thousand youth came forward at the end of the services for commitment and information. One of Dr. Graham's primary messages emphasized the importance of the community of believers, the strength and mutual benefit gained by staying connected to one another.

In the dungeons of Hanoi, men—especially those with religious convictions—discovered just how much they needed one another. Though many discussed differences in beliefs, their individual theologies paled in light of holding together under the most trying circumstances as men of faith and men of courage.

Jerry could feel his body weakening more and more with each passing year. He was not certain how much weight he had lost, but he knew it was considerable. His forearms, normally muscular, were shrinking: it made the large scorpion-shaped scar on his right arm even more prominent. Jerry rubbed his finger across the bumpy tissue.

When he was twenty, he had pitched every inning of a fast-pitch softball game despite having a four-inch gash sewn up just a few hours earlier. The deep cut was on his pitching arm, and during the game all the stitches had pulled out. *I probably wouldn't have the strength right now to pitch even one inning,* he thought, *stitches or no stitches.*

He looked down at his empty tin plate.

I am so thankful, God, that Terry and Tommy and little Lori will never have to experience hunger like this.

He wondered how much his children had grown. Tommy was nearly ten now and Lori almost seven, ready for school. He still had not been allowed to send or receive a letter, though many other POWs had been permitted to do so. The nightmare he first had experienced at the Zoo of his children drowning in a swift current and his desperate attempts to save them reccurred frequently. Each time he would wake up before the dream ended, always drenched in sweat.

My son is probably hungry all the time like I was as a boy, thought Jerry. He remembered when he would run into the house saying the familiar childhood mantra, "I'm starving!" He realized now he had never really known what hunger was before. He'd give anything for a piece of his wife's pecan pie and coffee. His body craved food all the time: sweets, fruits, and vegetables, but most of all, protein.

Rice always came with worms; soup always came cold—and often with something floating in it. Jerry thought back to the many times he had found an inch-long piece of fatback, complete with bristles. He would bite into the fatback in an effort to lend a little flavor to whatever he was eating but also to ingest at least a smidgen of protein.

On this particular morning, he noticed something new bobbing in his bowl: a very small whole fish, sun-dried and salted. He lifted it out with his fingers and looked at it a moment. It was about four inches long.

He put the entire fish in his mouth and held it. Jerry's saliva slowly dissolved the fish, and he was left with only a small ball of tiny bones. At least he had absorbed a little protein, and Will, gracious as usual, offered him the remainder of his water.

As he finished his soup that morning at the School, Jerry had just spit the ball of fish bones into his bowl when guards once again barged into the cell. They made rolling motions with their hands. He now knew exactly what this meant: roll up your mat and pick up your tin cup—it was time to relocate. And once more, the guards hauled Jerry and Will, both blindfolded, back to Hoa Lo Prison in downtown Hanoi.

After the V deposited him in his new location, Jerry realized he was back at Vegas. Guards led him to a corner cell, and in a few moments, the door opened. Will was pushed in too.

"Well, Will, here we are again," Jerry said. "Can you believe this space?" Jerry looked around at this new area. The larger cellblocks had been modified to smaller seven-by-nine-foot units containing two sets of narrow, wooden top-and-bottom bunk beds coarsely built with no mattresses. "Surely they won't add anyone else in here."

But as he turned around, turnkeys shoved two more POWs into the cramped space. Four grown men now shared a cell no bigger than a large closet—grossly cramped for two adults, insanely suffocating for four.

This new arrangement defined staying connected in totally different ways. What men had had to adjust to in solitary or in two-man cells now had to be relearned to accommodate several other people.

Jerry introduced himself to his new cellmates. They recognized each other's names from their communication through the walls. Everyone shook hands and began to arrange their meager possessions on the bunks: mats, cups, and thin cotton blankets. They quickly realized any activity done in the center space, which measured about twenty-four inches wide, would require other cellmates to be on their beds. If there were any idiosyncrasies, unusual habits, or other peculiarities of personality, all these would have to be accommodated, understood, and allowed for.

"So they are only giving us one toilet bucket to share?" one of his new cellmates asked, looking at the single two-gallon metal bucket about fifteen inches high with its thin, rusty rim, sitting in the corner. "This should be nice," he muttered.

Jerry began adjusting himself to several cellmates confined in an area with no space for living, merely existing. *It's not much different from being the youngest in a family of nine*, he mused, *except, of course, then I could just go outside and ride horses if I wanted to get away.*

The first evening together, the four pilots shared their stories of where and how they had been captured.

One of Jerry's new cellmates told about his shoot-down experience and being marched through the streets of Hanoi, where he was photographed by a number of international journalists. After the war, they learned one of these pictures had become an image known worldwide, representing all POWs and MIAs. It had been printed in newspapers and magazines and broadcast on televisions around the world.

"I crushed my arm on ejection," he told the others, "and it's never really healed properly." Jerry could easily see that his right arm was grossly disfigured, evidently broken and never reset, so it had mended at an angle and looked as if there were three elbows instead of one.

The other pilot had been shot down in 1966 and immediately had undergone extreme physical brutality that was intended to extract a confession for propaganda purposes. During this time period, the V often lit into new shoot-downs, counting on the trauma of their crash and capture to help elicit false statements. The new cellmate had been introduced to prison life in a trial by fire.

Though the cell was crowded, Jerry's need to pace continued. He asked the other men if they minded, since all three would need to be in their bunks while he used up the narrow center space. No one objected. They were all in weakened conditions due to inadequate food and various illnesses, including diarrhea and dysentery, but for Jerry, pacing helped him meditate. The others sometimes did push-ups or sit-ups on their wooden beds to try to maintain some semblance of physical strength.

As the days stretched on, one of Jerry's cellmates developed asthma. "Have you ever had this before?" Jerry asked him.

"Never," he said, "but I heard several other POWs are having trouble with it too."

After a few weeks his condition worsened. Now he was gasping for air nearly all the time, especially at night, and usually had to resort to sleeping sitting up. Jerry wished there was something he could do for his cellmate, but without proper medication, Jerry was powerless to provide assistance.

His cellmate's condition continued to deteriorate. Jerry watched as this man stood in the middle of the concrete floor at night between the bunk beds, which were no more than twenty-four inches apart. He would raise his arms and rest each elbow on a slat of the wooden steps nailed to the vertical posts of the beds. Because the beds were so close together, this position allowed him to suck in some air and doze a little at the same time, propped up between the ladders. It was the only time he got any sleep.

Jerry hated the feeling of helplessness, realizing his cellmate was struggling to stay alive. He labored for each breath. Sometimes at night the other three men wondered if he was going to make it until morning.

At the same time, the asthma caused a sniff as dependable as clockwork—innocuous in the beginning but maddening as time marched on.

While Jerry did his usual pacing one day between the bunks, he became aware of his cellmate's steady sniff. It seemed odd he had never noticed it before, but suddenly the sound amplified in his head as if with speakers. He tried hard not to focus on it in the seven-by-nine-foot space, but the harder he tried, the louder and more irritating the sniffing became. This went on day after day.

He tried to overlook the effect the noise was having on him.

He told himself how silly it was to let this bother him. No one felt more compassion than Jerry did for this man, battling for every breath.

Jerry prayed for patience. He tried to lessen its impact by counting the length of time between sniffs—anything to distract his mind from the constant noise. *One thousand one, one thousand two, one thousand three*—until he reached one thousand eleven . . . then *sniff.* And the whole sequence started all over again. Every eleven seconds, the cellmate sniffed. Jerry thought he was going to lose his mind.

One day Jerry, who already was gaining a reputation among prisoners for having the patience of Job—an officer with "infinite patience," as one of his SROs later described him in an official evaluation, whose "patience cannot be lost"—simply could go no longer without saying something.

In his usual, respectful demeanor, Jerry quietly said to the man suffering from asthma, "Do you realize you sniff every eleven seconds, round the clock, day after day, without stopping? Do you realize that? I am about to go up *this wall.*"

His cellmate, who was lying on his bunk, rose up slowly. In as measured a voice as he could muster, he looked steadily at Jerry and said, "Tom, do you realize that you whistle under your breath every day, day in and day out, especially when you're pacing? And I'm about to go up *that wall.*"

They both looked at each other . . . and burst out laughing.

■　■　■

During the time following Jerry's arrival back at Vegas, it soon became apparent why the North Vietnamese had remodeled this part of Hoa Lo Prison—to accommodate a burgeoning prisoner population. It was one of Jerry's current roommates who had come up with the name "Little Vegas," usually shortened to just "Vegas," and the name had stuck. He had done his pilot training at Nellis AFB just outside Las Vegas. As time went along, other POWs called separate areas within this sprawling part of the Hanoi Hilton by names of casinos on the Strip—Stardust, Desert Inn, Thunderbird, Riviera, Golden Nugget, the Mint.

During remodeling of new areas, the Vietnamese had taken extraordinary measures to stymie communication among increasing numbers of inmates. No two cells faced each other, and spaces between walls separated cellblocks. Windows contained additional slats, and any opening was covered over with bamboo mats.

Yet Vegas's labyrinth design and Vietnamese attempts to hinder prisoners' ability to communicate with one another only heightened the creativity of men determined to stay connected. Some POWs discovered metal drinking cups pressed against vertical surfaces amplified mere whispers enough to be heard through walls, even ones with narrow corridors between. In Jerry's cell, the men discovered tapping on the floor worked best for their cell. One POW noted that after lunch, when guards often napped and so much tapping commenced, it "sounded like a cabinet factory."

Tapping, however, was not the only means of communicating. Sometimes men wrote notes on tiny pieces of toilet paper using a pencil fashioned from bits of coal. If intercepted, these notes could bring severe punishment, so they were often passed by sticking them in a crevice in the wall or some other hiding place around the area where toilet buckets were emptied. Guards made an effort not to go too close because of the stench. As a result, this often was the safest method to communicate.

But there were other ways messages could be sent. Footsteps could be timed in such a way as to "pat out" a signal. Chests could be slapped, clothes thumped, brooms swept, plates banged—anything that could exhibit a visual signal or produce a noise had potential for sending a message. Howard "Howie" E. Rutledge, shot down on November 28, 1965—not long after Jerry—summarized the process succinctly and simply: "During those long years of captivity, we learned to communicate with anything and everything."

It was always perilous to stay connected, but it was always done.

A primary goal for POWs during the middle years of incarceration—a crucial reason to stay connected—involved tracking who had been captured and when. Jerry used a simple method of memorizing prisoners' names alphabetically using his knuckles. A man whose name began with *A* was on the top of his first knuckle, then the next name in alphabetical order was in the "valley," or space between the knuckles. The next name, again in the alphabetical order, sat on top of the next knuckle, then the next name down in the valley. He memorized hundreds of names using this method, and sometimes he would know whether he had skipped someone just by a last name being in the wrong place on his hands. He practiced the list two or three times every day. When a new shoot-down came in, he would have to insert this new name into the system and make appropriate adjustments with all other names using the knuckle-valley method. This was tedious and time consuming, but it worked for Jerry.

It was imperative for the POWs to maintain an accurate head count: they all knew any of them could easily disappear. The grossly unsanitary living conditions had taken their toll on everyone. Any cut or scratch was certain to fester; skin conditions developed, including boils, rashes, blisters, and sores. Many used urine to cleanse these areas. Some who developed ear infections poured their urine directly into ear canals in an attempt to kill bacteria. One in four was seriously ill or injured or both.

Often POWs entered captivity with broken bones. One POW who broke his leg while ejecting was told by an interrogator that if the leg became gangrenous, they would throw the leg along with him onto the garbage dump for burning. The POW said he had no doubt that would have happened.

In addition, there had been an escape attempt. The two escapees had been recaptured within a short period of time and both submitted to brutal beatings. One man survived; one did not. All POWs knew there existed a very real danger of guards not letting up once punishment began. With their isolated living conditions, it was imperative to do what they could to monitor as many as possible.

One of the ways Jerry tried to keep everyone informed of who was held in Vegas and who was not utilized their porcelain-covered tin plates and aluminum spoons. The Vietnamese enjoyed bragging that the POW spoons were stamped out from the salvaged metal skins of US airplanes they had shot down. Jerry turned these aluminum utensils to good advantage.

Guards often asked him to clean dishes after meals. This

was something of a misnomer since there wasn't any soap, and when there was, it was non-sudsing lye. Some men licked their plates completely clean, trying not to leave anything on them that might attract bugs and rats.

Jerry, however, saw this as an opportunity to relay names of men captured. By carving into the thin edges of their tin plates the last name and shoot-down date of a pilot, he preserved a record—sometimes the only record in prison which identified a man as POW rather than MIA. The family of Commander Bill Franke, who had taught Jerry the tap code at Heartbreak Hotel when he was first imprisoned, had been notified of his death and had had his funeral—only to find out later, much to their disbelief and joy, that Franke was not dead at all but alive and in captivity.

One day, Jerry heard an incredibly poignant story from one of his cellmates. The incident had occurred at Heartbreak.

"My cell door banged open one night," his cellmate said, "and the guards rushed in. I had heard 'through the walls' that they were working their way around, and I knew I was in for it—they were after any kind of confession or whatever they could get out of you. Man, I was really dreading it."

Jerry knew the feeling all too well. Sometimes POWs who had experienced torture previously would start shaking involuntarily when guards came for them—because they knew what was about to happen.

"I just felt so alone," he continued.

What happened next was a small incident by Hanoi Hilton standards, but in such a hostile environment, sometimes the small things loomed the largest.

"As the V were taking me down the corridor," he told Jerry,

"they had to stop in that narrow passage for something. And they had me shoved up against one of the cell doors."

Jerry remembered well the gloomy appearance of the interiors at Heartbreak. Dim lighting and putrid smells created a foreboding and unpleasant atmosphere.

"As I stood there waiting—didn't know if they were planning to put me in the 'ropes' or what—all of a sudden, I felt the finger of somebody gently touching the side of my foot from under the cell door I was leaning against." Jerry's cellmate stopped speaking a moment and looked down.

Their cell was quiet. Jerry and the others could imagine the scene.

"Do you know who touched your foot?" asked Jerry.

"No, I have no idea who it was," his cellmate said, regaining his composure. "But it was as if that guy was saying to me, 'You're not alone.' I really needed it right then."

As the days continued at Vegas, men did everything they could to support one another. They knew the widespread brutality. Sometimes Jerry heard anguished screams in other parts of the camp, but usually coming from the direction of the bath area.

Most POWs who had been captured early on, like himself, had not experienced outright torture during the first few months of their captivity. This gave time for them to get acclimated, to some extent—other Americans could get in touch with them as soon as possible, like how Commander Bill Franke had reached out to him at Heartbreak. It helped the new shoot-downs to feel they were a part of a network and therefore not completely alone.

However, during the middle years, often shoot-downs

immediately were subjected to a full-throttled torture session as soon as they arrived in Hanoi. Many had ejected, sustaining broken bones, one or two with broken backs. POWs already there in prison tried to get in touch with them as soon as possible to keep them from succumbing to depression and fear.

On one occasion, Jerry was sitting in his cell at Vegas when he heard someone screaming in the distance, then sobbing. He began to pray for whoever it was—he suspected it was a new guy just captured. Then he heard the man calling out in anguish, "God, please let me die!"

The cries wrenched Jerry's heart. He knew the man was suffering horribly. He prayed for him all day long. Staying connected meant doing all he could—and sometimes, it meant simply sitting and praying.

■ ■ ■

It began as an ordinary, monotonous morning for the prisoners in the Thunderbird building at Vegas. Suddenly, however, the day turned ominous. A message came "through the walls."

qzs . . . bios . . . ropes . . .

Jerry and his cellmates immediately dreaded what it meant: the V must be methodically working their way through the cells to obtain biographies. For some of the men in Vegas, this would be their first experience at straining to keep from writing a biography or confessions of war crimes. But Jerry knew what to expect—absolute viciousness.

For the moment, however, he had an even greater concern. What had he written before? When he had come out of the pit at Briarpatch, he gave misinformation in his biography to protect his family. Yet due to the diminished physical condition he had been in at the time, there was no way to remember now exactly what he had written then.

He had no more time to think about it. The cell door banged open. "You, Cuh, Cuh! You . . . now!" Jerry took deep breaths as two guards escorted him to the torture room.

The interrogator had him sit before him on a small wooden stool about fourteen inches off the ground. He explained to the prisoner that he would need to write a biography and comply quickly—they would not tolerate slowness.

Jerry sat still watching him. The interrogator's face was stony, his voice hard. Occasionally in a "quiz," a POW could sense if an interrogator might relent or go easy. That was not the case this time—Jerry knew he meant business.

"You Yankee air pirate! You will write biography." The interrogator waited for Jerry's response. Jerry paused and prayed.

"According to the Geneva Conventions, I don't have to do that," said Jerry.

Suddenly, the two guards on either side of him pulled his hands behind him and locked his wrists in metal cuffs and put him on his knees with a guard on either side.

"We want biography, Cuh! We want you write biography!" the interrogator said.

"According to the Geneva—" but Jerry never got to finish the sentence.

The guard on his right side raised his AK-47 and struck Jerry's cheek and ear with the butt of his rifle full force. Jerry collapsed, and excruciating pain surged through his face, especially his ear. For several seconds he couldn't see and struggled to regain some composure, his head ringing.

"Cuh, I not tolerate this! You will write!" barked the interrogator.

Jerry finally was able to rise into a sitting position. He simply shook his head slowly, and in the next seconds, guards began winding small cords around his left arm just above the elbow as tightly as they could. Then with the end of the cord, they pulled his left arm over to his right arm behind his back and wound the cords as tightly as possible just above the right elbow. Next, they pulled the two arms as close together as possible. Jerry could feel his shoulders straining under the intense pressure.

Within moments, however, the pain became numbness, and somehow the guards knew when that occurred. No sooner were both Jerry's arms and hands completely deadened from lack of circulation than guards quickly released the tension on the ropes and blood suddenly surged back into his arms with tremendous force. The intensity of pain was staggering.

Jerry screamed out. The "ropes" created the most debilitating sensations he had ever experienced in his life.

Sweat immediately poured from his head and chest. The guards seized him again. They wound the cords, tightening them as much as possible behind his back so that almost the entire length of his arms was touching, then allowed both his upper arms and hands to go completely numb and loosened the cords again. It sent shock waves through Jerry's entire body. His yelps were completely involuntary.

Through the next several hours, he couldn't form any specific prayer in his mind. All focus centered on the numbing, followed by the screaming explosion of blood tearing back into limbs that, by this time, were completely useless. His arms felt like they were about to burst from their shoulder sockets.

At some point, the guards began raising his arms up and over the back of his head. One guard placed his foot squarely into Jerry's shoulder blades to provide more leverage against bones and ligaments resisting the press upward. Now the POW was bent over, nose to knees, and could hardly catch a breath, his internal organs straining to function.

He vaguely thought about the first torture session he had endured in the pit: slow and deliberate. The "ropes" torture was a type of explosive brutality meant to force submission as quickly as possible.

Jerry was drenched, wet all over. He couldn't tell if it was just sweat. He suspected not.

Two or three days passed, maybe longer. He couldn't tell. He only knew he was reaching the edge of his mental faculties once again. He relinquished: pride and ego were matters that had little meaning under such circumstances.

"Bao Cao . . . Bao Cao," he was gasping for breath, nearly suffocating in the bent-over position. When guards untied his arms, he couldn't lift them. Finally, they helped him place his hands on the table and wrapped his fingers around a pencil. He was so weak he couldn't hold it. The interrogator rapped his knuckles on the table, then left the room for a while. Jerry put his head down on the desk.

Lord . . . God . . . help me write something. No idea what I said before . . . make this work. Oh God . . . help me . . .

When Jerry finally was taken back to his cell, his cellmates quietly watched him lurch through the door. He was beginning to get some return of feeling in his shoulders but remained weak all over. He looked terrible, pale and sweating, and his arms hung limp at his sides.

"Are you okay?" one of them asked tentatively. They were all concerned—and not just for him. They knew their time in the torture room would not be far off.

There was dead silence for several seconds. Jerry shuffled to his bunk, then raised his head to look at them. They saw on his face a glimmer of well-being untouched by the brutality he had just endured.

"Well," said Jerry slowly, "I guess you've got to expect a few losses some of the time."

His cellmates erupted into chuckles and helped him lie down.

That night as Jerry rested on his bunk, he wondered if the man he had heard scream several weeks before had been in that same torture room, perhaps enduring the ropes. He prayed again for him. And he prayed for all the POWs.

Lord, help me stay committed. We need each other more than ever. If I can help in some way . . . Keep all of us here in prison committed to our mission and committed to faith and country. Help me find a way to do that.

Jerry suddenly had to cough. When he did, he heard a distinctive wheezing sound swooshing out from his ear accompanied by a quick, sharp pain.

And, God . . . please heal my ruptured eardrum.

CHAPTER 13

A WAR OF WORDS

1969

AT NEARLY EVERY CAMP in the prison system of North Vietnam, propaganda spewed from cell loudspeakers daily. Generally, it began in the morning and lasted for several hours. The decibels were earsplitting, and guards usually wanted men to sit at the ends of their beds to listen. The propaganda always aimed toward one goal: articulating the fundamentally unfair and cruel governmental policies of the United States versus the fair and humane policies of Communist North Vietnam.

It always included a list of crimes committed against the Vietnamese people. The POWs were "warmongers," "Yankee air pirates," and "the blackest of criminals." Emphasis was placed on leniency of treatment if the prisoners would denounce the unjust actions of their country and submit to Vietnamese authority.

Day in and day out, cell loudspeakers blared indoctrination. Propaganda continually reiterated a single message: "The United States is an evil nation." Sometimes these statements would be read by a woman. Just as Japan had Tokyo Rose in World War II, Vietnam had Hanoi Hannah.

When a man was taken to the camp commandant's room, an interrogator would seek any statement that might be used as evidence the POW was turning against the United States or as evidence he was being well treated. Sometimes a long cloth draped over the wooden desk concealed a tape recorder underneath.

Often enough pressure was exerted that men were coerced into reading statements over the camp loudspeakers. POWs used devices to alert others this chore was done under duress. Mispronounced words or singsong presentations signaled they resented what they were being forced to do. Some exaggerated their accents or talked in a stuttering manner.

The various effects were humorous but also signaled continued opposition to the task. Sometimes mispronunciations of Vietnamese officials, especially the name Ho Chi Minh, received the greatest reaction. But men had to be extremely cautious, since the slightest hint of disrespect could bring swift reprisal.

One of the most unfortunate conditions of existence for the POWs, however, didn't come directly from the V but rather from the States: learning of the tremendous antiwar sentiment back home was demoralizing. The captors used stories of protests and riots to undermine morale and gain support for their cause. Most men stated, when they were released, that they had noticed a ramping up of mistreatment in prison paralleling the ramping up of antiwar sentiment in the States.

These announcements also frequently blared lists of Americans that were confirmed killed in action, which were recounted by name and hometown. Due to the language barrier, these sometimes produced a result more humorous than despairing.

For many weeks, Jerry and other cellmates kept hearing the lists of names. Occasionally, after the name would come this phrase: Chick-a-go-three. He and his cellmates kept looking at each other—what on earth could that mean? At last someone figured it out: Chick-a-go-three was actually Chicago, Ill. The POWs just shook their heads. Somehow it was part of the surreal experience each one of them faced.

Jerry smiled when he first realized what the mistaken translation really meant. Yet his levity passed quickly. The prisoner knew the mispronunciation represented grief back home.

Sometimes, however, POWs learned about current news events they would not have known otherwise. One day as Jerry sat on his bunk, the loudspeakers blared a propaganda statement with articles listed as "Even ifs."

"You blackest of warmongers! You criminals! Yankee air pirates! Even if United States have big army, big planes, we defeat you.

"Even if United States have more, we have soldiers who will win.

"Even if you have guns and weapons, we will defeat you.

"Even if you have universities and schools, we know more.

"Even if you have man who walk on moon . . ."

All four men in Jerry's cell looked up. "Did you hear that?"

"Wow! NASA finally got someone up there—wonder who it was?"

The monotony of the daily grind was sometimes relieved

in unexpected ways in the four-man cells. One morning, miscommunication combined with a lack of knowledge of the US military services produced a bright spot for everyone within earshot of the incident. It all began when a guard the prisoners called "Mouse" jerked open the small "judas window" set at eye level in the door of the four-man cell Jerry lived in.

"Conducting survey," said Mouse with pompous authority. The men in the cell remained motionless, two of them lying on their wood bunks, one sitting on the edge of his, the other standing against the wall.

"Cuh, are you Air Force?" he barked through the little window in the cell door.

"Yes," said Jerry quietly, not looking up or supplying any additional information that might provoke further dialogue. The Vietnamese knew as soon as they captured someone what branch of service he was in because of flight suit markings, so servicemen openly acknowledged that information.

Mouse proceeded to the next man and asked, "Fo, are you Air Force?" Will Forby answered yes, also not moving.

To the third man leaning against the wall, Mouse asked the same question, "Are you Air Force?" Again, a simple yes indicated the third man's branch of service.

There was only one man left in the cell. "Are you Air Force?" This man answered no, without further information.

Mouse stood still a moment. "Are you Navy?" The fourth cellmate was in fact an F-4 backseater with the Navy.

"Yes," the prisoner said without further elaboration.

Mouse slammed their judas window shut, and the four cellmates could hear him walking to the next cell door to continue his important survey.

As he progressed down the narrow corridor, Mouse's voice could be heard increasingly filled with the importance of his mission. "Conducting survey" began each encounter, and the prisoners would only answer yes or no without further elaboration, forcing Mouse to "discover" what branch of military service each prisoner was in.

Finally, Mouse could be heard around the corner from Jerry's cell, opening the judas window on one of the last cell doors in the building.

"Conducting survey," Mouse announced proudly. He began questioning the first man: "Are you Air Force?" The prisoner answered yes, and Mouse proceeded to the next man in this two-man cell.

Mouse began again with proud timbre, nearly at the end of this obviously significant task. "Are you Air Force?"

The last man to be surveyed said no.

Mouse's voice went up a notch. "Are you Navy?"

The prisoner answered no.

There was a momentary pause. When he next spoke, the guard's voice was louder and higher in pitch than ever. "Are you Army?"

He quietly said no.

Then, exasperated and confused, Mouse blurted out, "Why you here?"

His last survey participant was a Marine, a branch of service evidently unfamiliar to this particular Vietnamese guard. The eavesdropping American prisoners in surrounding cells buried their heads in whatever they could grab, desperately trying to muffle their laughter.

■ ■ ■

Jerry had been at Vegas over eighteen months now. His corner cell had a high window overlooking a small dirt yard with another cell opposite. Bamboo mats covered the window, but one of his cellmates had discovered early on that when he stood on top of his wooden bed and stretched, he could catch glimpses around the edges of the mats to the outside.

From this elevated vantage point, he could observe guards coming and going through the door of the facing cell, which they soon realized was a torture room. The restricted view hindered them from identifying clearly which POW they were seeing. But they could estimate, based on gait and demeanor, a POW's physical condition, particularly following torture.

One day, Jerry's cellmate suddenly looked around and said, "Hey, guys, I think I see Chester."

This was news indeed. "Chester" was the nickname of Commander James Bond Stockdale. Of course, Jerry knew who this was—they all did. He had been the senior-ranking officer of the entire camp: his bravery and strong leadership under incredible duress were already legendary to all POWs in captivity. For every blow Jerry might endure, Stockdale, who was known by the enemy to be an important commander in the US military, endured twenty.

Stockdale had been in isolation for the past eighteen months, best anyone could determine, and might possibly be back at Vegas. He walked with a permanent limp, the result of prolonged torture. The nickname came from the famous deputy of the hit TV series *Gunsmoke*, who also walked with a limp.

"Can you make out what's going on?" asked Jerry.

"Two guards led a guy with a bad limp into that cell. They came out pretty quickly, so they might just be letting him cool off for a while," his cellmate answered.

Immediately Jerry and his cellmates began a campaign to establish contact with the man in the torture cell whom they suspected might be Commander Stockdale. They located a small piece of torn toilet paper, stiff enough to be used as a signaling device from around the corner of the mat. They had to wait until siesta time though. Usually camp guards took a break after lunch from noon until about two. These were the safest times to attempt communication.

To use paper to send the tap code mimicked how it was done through the walls. Flicks of the paper, either up or down, counted to the row where the letter was contained. Then the next flicks would count across to the chosen letter. For example, if a man wanted to relay the letter *T*, he flashed the paper four times rapidly, then paused and flashed four times again.

By this time, Jerry and most of the POWs were so proficient with the tap code, no thinking was required. A man could simply hear the knocks or see the code flashed, yet he no longer counted; he simply knew what letters the sequences or taps represented.

His cellmate began a concerted effort to signal, *who r u.*

There was no response. A few minutes later he tried again. Nothing yet. Again. Jerry's cellmate had to keep an eye out for guards in the small yard while he bent down on the floor to see if anyone was patrolling in front of their own cell door. Jerry whispered, "Clear."

His cellmate flashed the message again. *who r u.*

This time they all heard a sustained cough that spelled out *cag*.

Those letters stood for "Commander, Air Group," designating Stockdale's command responsibilities of all aircraft and aircraft personnel aboard an aircraft carrier before he was shot down and captured. The abbreviated naval moniker also became his nickname in prison. Hearing from Commander Stockdale was news indeed.

Jerry's cellmates continued to monitor events across the yard from their window. Now Stockdale began flashing his fingers to start a "conversation." He wanted to know as much as he could about what was going on in the large camp called Vegas. Who was SRO? How many POWs? What kind of interrogations? What was happening?

They sent him all the information they had. CAG explained he had been in isolation for over eighteen months and felt out of the loop. He flashed to them the most important piece of information: *when i feel i can retake command will let u know.*

During the past year and a half, the number of prisoners had nearly doubled. Much was happening, especially since torture and brutality had ramped up. Having Stockdale back in the mix would benefit everyone. He was already a legend in Hanoi—as courageous and brave as any man in prison and a natural-born leader. It was good to know that he was "online" again.

The buildings in this rambling complex loosely formed an outer ring, with all activity done in the central courtyard. A bath and sink with faucet at one end allowed prisoners to wash clothes and dishes in nonpotable water. Located beside the sink and faucet was a cubicle sectioned off into five shower stalls with flimsy bamboo screens. Here hand signals could be used periodically over the tops of stalls.

Several weeks after Jerry's cell had discovered the return of Stockdale, turnkeys ordered Jerry to the makeshift wash area to rinse dishes. He considered it an opportunity for possible communication. On one occasion, as he stood over the sink, suddenly from inside one of the adjacent cells came a husky voice. "This is Stockdale. Who are you?" Jerry turned toward where he thought the loud, hoarse whisper was originating, but the cell wall prohibited him from seeing the man. Before Jerry had time to answer, the impatient voice quickly croaked out once more, "It's Commander Stockdale. Who are you?"

Jerry quickly identified himself. "Captain Tom Curtis, shoot-down, 20 September, 1965."

Without further introduction, Stockdale launched into a directive he called BACK-US. Using the words as an acronym, he explained what it meant: *B* stood for "don't bow," meaning do not show subservience in any way to the enemy if possible; *A*—"don't go on the air," meaning do not make any recordings or broadcasts if possible; *C*—"don't admit to crimes or accept gifts," meaning be careful when interrogated and do not admit to war crimes or piracy of any type, regardless of bribes; *K*—"don't kiss good-bye," meaning do not show signs of friendship when leaving; and *US* stood for "unity over self."

Then Stockdale said to Jerry, "Get this out to everyone you can. Now repeat it!"

Jerry said, "BACK-US."

"No, no. *What does it stand for?*" Stockdale's gruff voice was filled with impatience again.

Jerry recited the acronym with the commander's help. Later

that day he began a concerted effort to relay through the walls Stockdale's order. If POWs could stand together, they had a better chance of enduring the incredibly difficult circumstances facing them.

Not long after this encounter with Stockdale, Jerry and others in his cell were approached by a Navy pilot through the walls about the possibility of joining a highly secretive group of POWs who would participate in learning a complex messaging system. If successful, it would connect with intelligence sources in the Pentagon. The mission was classified top secret at the highest level.

The small encrypted messages would be embedded in letters sent out from the prison if—or when—the POWs were allowed to write. It would also involve receiving letters from family members who had been contacted by officials in Washington, then decoding the messages planted within their letters. In order to be prepared in the event POWs could send and receive letters required great diligence in learning the code, especially since it was done through the walls.

Under normal circumstances, if a person could sit with a letter, reading it slowly and carefully in order to decipher its contents, the task would be doable. But these POWs knew guards would allow only a few moments with each letter—so that the system of counting words, looking at ending vowel combinations, and decoding would have to be done lightning fast. And if guards ever suspected such a system existed, their lives would be in jeopardy. They would be classified as spies and could be executed on the spot—no questions asked.

It was such a secretive group of participants that, for the most part, no one knew who else was involved in the covert operations except for the person who had been your primary contact. As Jerry contemplated the mission, he thought about the consequences of participating. But he also remembered the small touch underneath the door his cellmate had described to him: the desperate attempt of a man relating to another in hellish circumstances. He remembered the unknown man who cried out to God in torment, begging to die.

As Jerry prayed about possible involvement in such a program, he decided he had the temperament and desire to volunteer. And because of his growing reputation within the prison walls as a strong resister and someone who could be trusted, he was accepted immediately into the clandestine operation.

The name of constructing such a coded letter was "mixing a martini," referring to the scrambling of letters within a written piece. And Jerry began the tedious task of learning the complicated messaging system of a code within a code. Only time would tell whether he would have an opportunity to implement it.

At this point, Jerry had not been allowed to receive anything at all from Terry. The North Vietnamese would have to allow receipt of correspondence before the messaging system could be arranged. But he was willing. He knew the risks involved, and he accepted them. Because of incredibly inhumane treatment within the prison walls—and this treatment deteriorating daily—he felt it was the best way to make a contribution toward staying connected with military sources at home.

Perhaps some good will come of it, Lord—if I am ever allowed to send and receive letters from home . . .

CHAPTER 14

COMMITTED

1970

IF CIRCUMSTANCES TURNED a corner, most POWs after their release agreed it occurred toward the end of 1969. Developments in Washington—including the inauguration of a new president and progressing peace talks in Paris, though often in fits and starts—seemed to indicate a pivotal juncture. But the most significant event may have been the death of the Communist revolutionary leader who had become president of the Democratic Republic of Vietnam, Ho Chi Minh, on the morning of September 2, 1969.

Ho's passing brought guards into prison compounds the following day visibly subdued and grief stricken. During the next few weeks, there was a noticeable lifting of the strictest regulations. A third meal consisting of a half cup of reconstituted milk laced with sugar and a piece of bread provided additional calories; guards began allowing prisoners into the open dirt courtyards, sometimes without shackles; men were provided extra blankets; and a few received baskets with cloth linings to keep water warm for tea or instant coffee.

One POW, when served cabbage with a few chopped tomatoes plus seasoning on top—cooked just the way his wife prepared it back home—thought for sure it meant the war was over. In later years, when he smelled a similar dish cooking on his home stove, he would lift the lid off the pot and exclaim to his wife, "Look, the war's over!"

Though physical reprimand always lurked around the corner and several servicemen would experience additional solitary confinement, these events in the United States and North Vietnam combined to bring about improved treatment for POWs throughout the system during the early seventies. They indicated nothing, however, in terms of determining how much longer imprisonment would continue.

For over two years, Jerry was imprisoned at Vegas, until late 1969. Two more Christmases, two more years of family birthdays and anniversaries had been celebrated back home without him. Time was passing, but not for him. In prison, it seemed to stand still. A few months after Ho's death, guards culled more than fifty POWs from Vegas, including Jerry; loaded them into trucks, blindfolded and handcuffed; and transported them to a compound dubbed "Camp Hope." It would be remembered always by the entire prison population all across North Vietnam for one spectacular event—and for one very special reason to Jerry personally.

. . .

Jerry was discouraged. Many POWs, including himself, wondered if their country had forgotten them. It had been quiet in the skies for a long time—no bombing raids, no fighters roaring: not the sound of a single plane over Hanoi for nearly two years.

Camp Hope, also known as Son Tay, was a remote camp positioned some twenty-two miles northwest of Hanoi. In the long building where Jerry was located, guards locked him into a small one-man cell at night. The two-man cell next to him housed Will Forby plus another POW. During the day, guards would unlock both cell doors and allow the three men to mingle in the small interior space in front of the cells. They still were never allowed outside.

Men speculated as to why the V would make such a move at this point in the war, and many hoped against hope it might be a good sign—that the Communists would want to protect some of their prisoners, to make sure they stayed alive and were not killed should bombing commence again in Hanoi. But there was no way to know.

Jerry had just spent his fifth Christmas in captivity. It was inconceivable to him that he had been in North Vietnam that long. His son would be twelve years old in just a few weeks, and his daughter soon would be nine. He wondered if they liked school, what activities they enjoyed. He couldn't imagine what his children looked like now. And he missed his wife. He thought about the last time he held her just before he had left for Thailand: all that seemed forever ago.

But Jerry also was aware of his own aging. He would turn

thirty-eight later in the year. He was gaining back some weight. Since Ho's passing, POWs were being given a little more food—that was at least a positive. However, he knew there were several medical issues that needed tending.

First, his feet continued to be a problem. At Briarpatch, he had contracted beriberi, a condition resulting from vitamin deficiency, and his feet bothered him nearly daily—they burned like fire and were so sensitive, he couldn't stand for anything to touch them, not even thin cotton. A couple of years previously, he had broken one of his molars on a small rock in his rice. Since then, it had abscessed two or three times a year. During these bouts, he had to sleep sitting up to try to relieve the painful pressure from swelling and to aid in drainage.

Although nearly everyone else in the prison population had been permitted to receive correspondence, this was a privilege Jerry had not yet been allowed. Maybe it was because he had been a tough resister, never capitulating to his captors' demands without a struggle; maybe it was just coincidence. Whatever the reason, it amounted to prolonged punishment.

One morning as he paced in his cell at Camp Hope, a guard came up to the window opening and gave a chopping motion to his wrist, signaling to Jerry to put on his long-sleeved shirt. Jerry knew what that meant—he was about to be taken to the interrogator's room.

"Cuh, you come," he said to Jerry.

What do they want from me now? Jerry wondered.

He followed the guard into a cramped interrogation room. Behind the desk sat the camp commandant, holding a small piece of paper.

"Cuh, you blackest of criminal and you Yankee air pirate—you deserve nothing. But I be generous to you—even though you not deserve," he said. He continued to hold the paper.

"This letter . . . I allow you to read. But hurry! Not allow long." The camp commandant slowly laid the paper down on the desk in front of Jerry. Jerry immediately recognized Terry's handwriting. The commandant continued his rambling. The prisoner hardly noticed.

"Dear Jerry, How are you?" His eyes filled—he couldn't hold back. Jerry carefully touched the corners of the paper: a faraway world materialized before him.

"We are all just fine—busy with school and church activities. Tommy and Lori are doing so well in school. Growing so tall and the best news, they both have asked Jesus to come into their hearts." Jerry was weeping openly now, though silently, his shoulders quietly shaking. He could hardly see to read the last sentence.

"We miss you so much and love you more than you know. Terry."

The commandant snatched the paper up from the desk. "You go back to cell now." Jerry never saw the letter again. It didn't matter. God had given him a reason to stay committed.

When he got back into his cell, he fell to his knees in thanks.

Now that Jerry had been allowed to receive a letter from home, he began a steady campaign to send one to his wife. Once he was given permission, he used the opportunity to produce small encrypted messages within the letter using the system of coding he had been taught at Vegas.

He laughed to himself, thinking how funny it would sound to Terry—the code sometimes produced odd sentences. But since he knew other POWs within the clandestine unit had already sent his name to US intelligence authorities as a participant, he recognized they would contact her about the messaging—more than likely they already had done this.

In order to "mix a martini," Jerry had to memorize the content he would write and what words he would use before he arrived in the camp commandant's room to compose a letter.

From this point forward, the letters Terry and Jerry sent back and forth were coded; they still were allowed to exchange only a handful of letters each year. It didn't lessen the wonderful fact that they were now in communication. But the encrypting system did birth some strange-sounding English, such as "Being nostalgic at Christmas is a blessing" or "Please insure to maintain a good photo album."

When Terry wanted to write to Jerry, she would first send her letter to the Pentagon. The letter would be reworded to include the encryptions within her existing sentences. Then the letter would be returned to Terry to recopy in her own handwriting. She used preprinted paper cards provided to families by North Vietnam. The slips of paper were addressed to "Camp of Detention for U.S. Pilots Captured in the Democratic Republic of Vietnam," with strict instructions only to speak of "health and family."

For Jerry, receiving a letter from Terry was the intense part of the system. After the letter arrived, guards allowed him only a few minutes to see it, and then always under supervision. The encryption had to be deciphered on the spot, a nerve-racking task requiring complex decoding.

These secret messages allowed military authorities to obtain a better understanding of the living conditions and torture men were enduring, the names of prisoners, especially some still not accounted for, promotions within the ranks, and possible vulnerabilities of camps that might be useful should a rescue attempt be planned.

The bits of information were admittedly small, but for men living in darkness, any help they were able to offer provided something to strive toward. Jerry's clandestine involvement in the letter messaging system made him and the other POWs who participated feel they were at least contributing to the war effort, even if only one or two sentences at a time.

■ ■ ■

In July 1970, Jerry and all the prisoners at Camp Hope were transported to another facility about nine miles northwest of Hanoi. This would be the first time since Jerry's imprisonment that a large group of men were allowed to live together within the same cellblock. Seventeen other Americans were in Jerry's cell. Here he was the senior-ranking officer, though in some cases only by a few days, and therefore in charge of and responsible for the men under him. The POWs dubbed their new rural prison "Camp Faith." It was Jerry's ninth time to be moved since entering captivity in 1965.

Guards allowed men at Camp Faith outside for about thirty minutes each day. This was the first time in five years Jerry had been allowed outdoors and unshackled within the prison walls, except when escorted back and forth to the shower a time or two a month. Though brief, these sessions were a blessing.

In addition, men were being given a bit more to eat, so many were regaining strength. Several decided they would learn to do handstands.

"Hey," said one of Jerry's cellmates, "how about spotting for me?" The fellow prisoner wanted Jerry to stand in front of him and hold his hands up around his feet to keep him centered.

"Sure," said Jerry.

Several handstands later, somebody called out Jerry's name, and he turned to answer, an unfortunate circumstance for the would-be gymnast in the middle of his next handstand. He lost his balance and tumbled down hard.

"Oh my—sorry about that," Jerry said as he helped his cellmate to his feet. As they laughed about it, Jerry watched out of the corner of his eye one of his other cellmates surreptitiously picking up something from the dirt. Jerry knew what he was doing but kept quiet.

Two or three in Jerry's group had begun making plans to build a crystal set radio—a type of simple radio for receiving frequency waves. If planning an escape, it could be a useful tool for monitoring incoming messages.

The men scrounged the ground around buildings while they were outside. They managed to collect small pieces of wire, a few nails, and other odds and ends buried in the dirt, trash remnants from the original camp-construction activities. A few managed to remove razor blades from the bath area when guards weren't looking.

It was imperative these be kept hidden since reprisals would be fierce if the materials were found: inspections by guards were unannounced and always thorough. Usually only a few men at a time participated in such planning because, generally speaking, the fewer people that were involved, the better. That way, should the guards place pressure on someone, he could not give accurate information under torture.

Every POW in North Vietnam knew the story of the two airmen who had planned an escape for months and did in fact break out of their prison camp. They were caught almost immediately since they had no contacts outside the prison walls and, as Westerners, no way of blending into the surrounding population.

When they were brought back into the camp, both were beaten mercilessly. One of the men died during the brutal pummeling. Not only this, but after they finished with the two POWs who perpetrated the escape, guards instituted a systematic sweep through every cell, torturing the entire prison population, one at a time, as camp-wide retribution for the attempt. The POWs were careful what they did and who they shared it with.

Jerry, as SRO for his group of seventeen men at Camp Faith, knew about the plans. This type of activity, though dangerous, had its positive side. He knew it gave them something to think about and plan for, taking their minds off imprisonment, even though guards would hold him responsible if anyone was caught.

■ ■ ■

Jerry suddenly jerked awake. At first he thought he was hearing things, but immediately the sound of gunfire in the distance commenced again. It was the middle of the night on November 20, 1970.

"Do you hear that?" he asked the guy sleeping next to him.

"Yes . . . what do you think?" the man said. Already several of the POWs in his cellblock had moved toward the shuttered windows to see if they could glimpse anything.

"I think I see some flashes of light out west of us, out toward

Son Tay," one airman said. This group of prisoners had been evacuated from there a little over three months before. Suddenly the unmistakable sound of US jet fighter cover meant to create a diversion came screaming overhead.

One of the younger and newer POWs turned with a questioning look to Jerry.

"I just don't know," he said, "but something's happening for sure." He didn't want to pose any speculations that might be false, but before he nodded off again that night, a small glimmer of hope awakened in his thoughts. He felt in his bones that something significant was going down—there just wasn't any way to know for certain.

Within a day or so, guards rushed into their cells, waving rifles and yelling frantically. They hastily packed up Jerry and his men with their belongings and loaded them onto trucks. The speeding vehicles took all of them back to downtown Hanoi and into the large Hanoi Hilton once more, into an area of the camp POWs began calling "Camp Unity."

When Jerry and the men under him arrived back at the Hilton, they were deposited into a large building just as Vietnamese prisoners were being led out. This building was one of several large bay-style cellblocks loosely ringing a central courtyard.

Jerry's group now found themselves with most of the other men who also had been at Camp Faith but in separate areas. Approximately forty-five men were locked in this cell about twenty by sixty feet in size. In the middle of the cell, a concrete platform elevated about four inches off the floor served as a sleeping area. It covered virtually the entire center portion of the cell. Each man had about eighteen inches sleeping space on these concrete beds.

As they were being shuffled into their new large cellblock in Hanoi, they heard other trucks and commotion: men being unloaded all over the complex. The buildings in this part of the Hanoi Hilton compound usually held only Vietnamese prisoners. Now the buildings seemed to house only American POWs. Certainly something was happening.

But regardless of why all of them were suddenly brought back into Hanoi, that first evening held unbelievable joy. Being united in large groups for the first time brought a wellspring of pent-up emotions to the surface. Though most of Jerry's large group had been at Camp Faith, they had not all been together in the same cell. Before, only eighteen men, including himself, were in his unit. Now it was remarkable to see forty-five POWs who had been imprisoned elsewhere together under one roof. He suspected the other buildings were experiencing the same pandemonium.

Still, each building only represented a fraction of the total prison population. They were not allowed to mingle together as an entire group, and they now estimated several hundred men were POWs in North Vietnam. At Camp Unity, the men numbered these buildings. Jerry's was labeled Big Room 3.

Within the next few days, however, a major bit of information spread like wildfire through the walls of Unity and became the subject of hours of speculation. It explained many things, including why every POW from outlying camps had been rushed in frenzied haste back to Hanoi.

Jerry was speechless when he first heard about it. "You say he saw a drawing of what?" he asked the POW explaining to him what had just been transmitted through communication channels.

"This guy over in one of the other cellblocks said he was using the latrine when all of a sudden this stick came through the window," said the POW, his excitement visibly animating his face.

In these big rooms at Camp Unity, primitive communal latrines were located in the corner of each cell with a barred window to the outside.

"You're kidding! You mean he was just standing there, and a stick came in between the bars?" asked Jerry.

"Yes! And it had a piece of paper stuck to the end of it. So the guy took the paper—had no idea what in the world was going on," the POW continued, "and it turned out it was from one of the Vietnamese prisoners."

At Camp Unity, the V held many allied Vietnamese prisoners together in a separate cellblock. Their ability to understand what guards were saying and talking about was an advantage for the Americans.

"The piece of paper had on it a crudely drawn compound-like structure. But it also had what looked like several parachutes coming down! The Vietnamese POW must have heard guards talking about it. That can only mean one thing! There must have been some kind of an attempted rescue at one of the camps by our Special Ops. Can you believe it?"

By now Jerry was as excited as the POW telling about it.

He turned to other guys who had been with him at Camp Faith.

"Hey . . . you guys remember that night we heard the firefight in the distance coming from Son Tay—I'll bet that has something to do with this," said Jerry.

The speculation began. And as military men, understanding

how these things work, they surmised it might be the very reason why the V had moved all men from outlying camps back into Hanoi so hurriedly. They wanted to make sure no one was rescued from their prisons. Hoa Lo Prison was the best fortified and least likely place for Americans to attempt a rescue operation.

As Jerry and the men who had been at Camp Faith with him remembered the night they had heard the fireworks plus jet-fighter cover coming from the direction of their previous camp, they realized what had happened. There must have been an attempted rescue of POWs at Son Tay in the middle of the night by US Special Ops forces.

Since he had been living at that camp just prior to the rescue attempt, he would have been one of the fortunate POWs liberated from Communist North Vietnam—except for one minor detail. The V had relocated him and the others just a few months before, so there were no POWs to rescue.

Nonetheless, Jerry's spirits soared in a way he had not experienced in six years—because it meant his country had not forgotten the POWs after all. It meant that despite all the reports of protests against the war in America, it meant despite all the celebrities from the States who had visited the camps and reported back to the homeland that things were rosy, it meant that even if many all over the world didn't support the war— nonetheless, his government had not deserted them. The news gave him a much-needed boost; all the others felt the same when they heard about it.

Though initial reports were sketchy, it was enough information for these military men to put the pieces of the puzzle together. And as new shoot-downs entered the prison, more and more details surfaced. The story gradually unfolded.

A joint group of volunteers from Army Green Berets and Air Force Special Operations had formed a top-secret contingency to participate in the daring mission. After many months of grueling preparation and acting on intelligence gathered from several different sources, six helicopters lifted off from Udorn, Thailand, heading toward the remote camp known as Son Tay (Camp Hope), located several miles west of Hanoi.

Special Ops forces executed their mission to perfection—the only problem they encountered was believing their eyes when they discovered no American prisoners in the compound at Son Tay around midnight, November 20, 1970. They were certain POWs had been there . . . but they were not there anymore.

For many minutes, everyone involved with the operation was in disbelief. Author John Gargus, in his book documenting the raid, records the stunned reaction of the rescuers who were finding merely empty cells:

> The scene inside the compound was incredible. No one believed what he saw and heard. "Negative items!" (Item was a code word for POW.) That was impossible! As level-headed and reliant on his men as [Captain Dick] Meadows was, he asked them to repeat their initial reports and then urged them to search again. That stunning revelation and disbelief went all the way up the chain of command. . . . Did everyone hear it right? As ridiculous as it may seem today, when the raiders were told to search the cells again, they did it in spite of the obvious results. They all hoped that the men they came to rescue would somehow reappear in their abandoned cells. [Captain Dan H.] McKinney

was dumbfounded. He had a long lanyard with a loop for every expected prisoner. He had hoped to be the man who would personally greet each freed man. He would look into his eyes, exchange a word or two to determine his condition, and then place one of the loops on his wrist to ensure that he was now in friendly custody. It just couldn't be happening!

When Jerry heard about the courageous rescue attempt, he realized it was indeed what he and his men had heard that night in November—the firefight in the distance, coming from the direction of Camp Hope, and the fighter jets screaming over them obviously providing diversionary cover. It explained why he and almost all POWs in outlying camps had been frantically moved back into downtown Hanoi. The V did not want to lose any of their prized captives to possible future rescue missions.

But Jerry's jubilation over news of what men were already calling the Son Tay Raid was short lived. When guards had moved prisoners so hastily back to Hanoi, the men under Jerry's command did not have time to destroy their scrounged crystal set radio parts. Unfortunately for Jerry, the V discovered the stash.

Word was sent to the camp commandant at Hoa Lo in Hanoi. Immediately, Jerry's old nemesis, Bug, set out to extricate him from the cell. As soon as the doors burst open, Jerry knew. They jabbed him with their rifles and roughly marched him out of Big Room 3, yelling at him incessantly.

He had no idea where they were taking him—somewhere in the vast expanse of Hoa Lo Prison. Various large compounds filled the Hanoi Hilton, and by this time, Jerry was well acquainted with most of them. But not where they took him this time.

Guards led him to a small room where an interrogator waited, along with two handlers known to be part of the torture squads. Jerry's body reacted the way all POWs who had endured previous physical punishment did: his heartbeat quickened, his muscles tensed up.

The camp interrogator was furious. Not only were authorities under pressure resulting from the Son Tay Raid attempt, but anxiety over what might happen next played a key role in their current bad moods.

"We find forbidden things—contraband. You leader, you responsible, Cuh. We punish you." The commandant spoke as one who knew he was standing on solid ground. The captive had been caught; now he must face the consequences.

Over the next few days, Jerry experienced the debilitating pain of torture once again. Forced to "hold up the wall," Jerry was required to stand away from the wall with arms raised, hands leaning against the wall holding up his weight, indefinitely. When he could no longer hold his arms up, he was forced to kneel on bare kneecaps on the concrete.

After a period of time, Jerry decided not to punish himself anymore and fell over. When he did, guards on either side pulled him up by the hair and forced him to continue to kneel. Now, not only was he bearing his own weight but the weight of the guards as well. His knees were raw.

He prayed under the increasing torment.

God . . . please, God. Help me survive. Help me. Let me live. Give me strength to endure.

After the guards had satisfied themselves that they had

delivered enough punishment for unauthorized contraband, they led Jerry, limping and exhausted, to a tiny, filthy, stand-alone cell.

This place is so isolated, I could scream my head off and no one could hear me, thought Jerry. He stretched out on his mat on the concrete floor, hurting all over, especially his knees. It was the middle of winter, Christmastime—his sixth in captivity. After having a taste of living in large groups, he knew solitary was really going to be difficult—and there was no way to know how long he would be there. He missed his family more than ever.

Jerry grappled with the darkness. He prayed for strength to endure, to stay the course, to continue to hang on, to remain committed.

God, I've been in North Vietnam now almost six years. It's been so long. Thank you so much for those brave men who came to Son Tay to try to rescue us. At least we know our government has not forgotten about us. God, that rescue attempt gave me hope. Please help me continue to persevere.

He went to sleep that night tired, cold, lonely. His recurring dream of attempting to rescue his children from deep waters returned during the night.

■ ■ ■

A few days later, a guard abruptly swung open his cell door. This guard was nicknamed "Gap" because of a wide space between his front teeth. Larger than most of the guards and somewhat dapper, he also showed no agreeable side to his nature. In fact, many had suffered in his hands during physical punishment.

As Jerry saw who had opened his door, he immediately felt unnerved. Long years of captivity had taught him to be highly suspicious of any change in schedule or activity. "Out, out." Gap motioned the prisoner outside.

Jerry walked through the doorway. This cell had three concrete steps down from the door to the ground, and there at the bottom sat a three-gallon tin tub filled with water. "Wash, wash," said the guard.

Jerry was so cold, he couldn't think of anything worse at that moment. In North Vietnam, the temperatures in winter seldom drop below freezing, but low forties and fifties seem frigid without any heat or heavy clothing, and especially when you are surrounded by cement walls and floors. But he was filthy and knew he needed to clean himself up—to at least make an effort.

When he reached his hand down into the water, he couldn't believe it. In fact, he was shocked. The water was warm—not hot, but certainly warmer than any shower or water he had used since becoming a POW. Since Jerry's solitary cell was located close to the kitchen, perhaps the water was leftover from kitchen workers performing cooking chores. When Gap saw they needed to empty the used water, maybe he ordered Vietnamese workers to carry the heavy bucket to Jerry's cell door in an unusual moment of compassion. Whatever the reason, the grungy captive was more than willing to accept it. Used warm water was better than no warm water at all.

Jerry grabbed his tin cup and began to pour the soothing liquid all over his head and face, one of the best sensations he could imagine. One cupful at a time, he splashed the tepid water all over his dirty feet and hands. Though the air around him remained frigid and the temporary warmth only accentuated the cold, he was so grateful for that one warm, brief bath.

CHAPTER 15

THE HANOI HILTON "UNIVERSITY"

SPRING 1971–SPRING 1972

DURING 1971 AND 1972, there remained a test of wills between captors and captives. Of course, guards continued to demand ridiculous shows of subservience, and there remained the threat of punishments. But for the most part, the brutality of the torture era was past. Now came a time of a different sort of adjustment: huge numbers of men with strong personalities living in extremely cramped spaces.

Jerry had spent his sixth Christmas confined again in solitary. After three cold winter months, he returned in spring 1971 to his large living group in Big Room 3 at Camp Unity. There he discovered one of the most rewarding developments possible: an amazing system for continued education had been initiated among the prisoners. It couldn't have come at a better time, so welcome after the weeks he had just endured.

When Jerry was imprisoned at Camp Faith, the POWs there had begun informal classes as a way to renew and stimulate their minds. Once men were living together in larger groups at Camp Unity, each cellblock began organizing classes, clubs, and groups that developed into what they would come to call the "university."

One of the POWs had been an experienced educator before prison. He was tasked with launching the learning program. Men were canvassed, then organized according to what they knew and could teach. Every cell had resident experts in a wide variety of subjects. Within days, a diverse curriculum of courses covering an amazing variety of subjects emerged.

Among the languages offered were French, Spanish, German, and a short course in Russian. Math was taught, including advanced calculus. The arts were not left out. Many had musical backgrounds and began figuring out ways to teach music fundamentals without instruments or recordings.

Electives included a variety of history, science, and electronics courses. A former member of the faculty at the Air Force Academy taught thermodynamics; another POW lectured on government and American history; an avid Civil War buff taught seminars covering every battle from start to finish. One POW had been a business major in college and taught business and accounting. Yet another POW had worked as a butcher and taught meat cutting. Someone else, whose hobby was wines, led his group on imaginary wine-tasting tours in France and Germany, teaching them the differences between all sorts of varieties, from cabernets to pinot noirs, solely by vivid descriptions of taste, color, and body. Beekeeping and diesel maintenance rounded out the offerings.

As Unity's educational system grew, one of the POW instructors noted later that all the typical complaints over workload, scheduling conflicts, and exam preparedness became a natural part of the process. Those who struggled with difficult material sought after-hours tutoring. "It was, in all the essential ways, a real school. Certainly learning was taken seriously, and the appetite for knowledge was great."

Naturally, disputes occasionally arose as to the facts stated in a given course. With nearly five hundred men spread among the various buildings, most college graduates and many with advanced degrees, there were always those willing to instruct and help with fact-checking.

But without the benefit of textbooks, memories often differed. The communications network would then get busy to see if there was someone else in another cellblock who could settle the matter. Of course, this had to be done through urgent tapping on the walls to another large cell group while students waited for the correct answer.

Sometimes, however, issues were settled on the basis of "most likely" or "strongest possibility." These cases were dubbed "Hanoi facts," meaning everyone would agree on a consensus "educated guess." Often these disputes continued until men returned home and could, at last, verify a specific bit of information. Sometimes, fairly large sums of money exchanged hands due to verification of disputed "Hanoi facts" once home.

The greatest handicap was lack of paper, pencils, blackboards, and reference books—all the natural accompaniments to most teaching environments. Without these supplies, men used only their memories and speech to relay learning.

As the men in Big Room 3 welcomed Jerry back from his

three-month stint in solitary confinement, they filled him in on everything that had happened while he was gone, who the new shoot-downs were, who had been sick, and who seemed to be experiencing more than the usual depression.

They also related to him what he had missed at Christmas. During the holiday celebration, POWs had exchanged imaginary gifts. Will Forby was given a life-size photo of Jerry to commemorate their sixth Christmas in prison together.

They then introduced Jerry to the "university" classes, now in full swing. It was nothing short of fabulous for him and filled a void—a need deep within for learning.

Since Jerry had joined the Air Force when initial sign-up required only a two-year minimum of college, he was in the minority among the POW population, most of whom had already graduated from four-year programs. He had always intended to complete his undergraduate degree at some point while in service, but the war and captivity interrupted all that. Having the opportunity now to further his education and intellectual development inspired him. He plunged in wholeheartedly.

Even before Camp Unity, Jerry had practiced Spanish and French "through the walls" for several years. By manufacturing ink using ashes or brick dust and water and forming a stylus from a bamboo sliver, he would write vocabulary words on pieces of toilet paper and memorize them. Then at Camp Faith, one of his cellmates spoke Spanish fluently, and another French, which continued his education.

Now, in Big Room 3, he discovered great teachers in both languages and immersed himself in their classes. He had chosen Spanish primarily because being from Texas, he already knew a respectable sprinkling of words and phrases. He studied French mainly because he enjoyed the sound of the language.

After attending study groups in both languages for more than eighteen months, he acquired a vocabulary of around four thousand words in each. He could converse at a relatively high level in both, but especially Spanish.

Another area of interest for Jerry was public speaking. He had always enjoyed teaching Bible classes in church, and standing before people to speak came easily to him. Several of the men formed a Toastmasters Club and gave speeches in front of the group, then were critiqued. Jerry joined the club. His speech on "How to Make a Louisville Slugger Bat" received a stunned ovation when he finished.

Will Forby also had been at Camp Faith and participated in studying Spanish there. Now he continued foreign language studies and sat in on business management. Neither pilot, Jerry nor Will, had any idea God was laying a foundation for each of them in prison to experience second careers later in life.

■ ■ ■

Before men were moved into larger living groups, one of the ways to pass time and keep minds active consisted of playing games. Someone fashioned a backgammon board by laminating layers of coarse toilet paper with rice-paste glue. The center of a small bread loaf—if the POW was willing to sacrifice bites of food—could be rolled and shaped into small disks to form game pieces. If he wanted to create checkers, red brick dust could be used to color one set red, and black coal dust could be used for the other set. Of course, anything of this sort had to be kept extremely small so it could be concealed quickly.

"Five Questions" became a favorite trivia-wagering game among POWs. Sometimes when answers were contested, bets ensued. Several men after their release sent money to other former POWs for wagers lost during contested games.

Occasionally, once the Vietnamese allowed prisoners to receive packages from home, someone might get a deck of cards. Before that, guards gave out a few decks of Vietnamese cards made from pasteboard glued together in thin layers. These couldn't be shuffled in regular fashion because they creased so badly, even breaking, so cards were mixed gingerly.

Playing bridge was by far the most complicated pastime. The four men making up a rubber often were not in the same cell or even adjoining cells. A hand of bridge might last two to three weeks since every move had to be tapped through a successive series of walls.

Jerry had never played cards, and one of the Navy pilots living with him in Big Room 3 noticed he was not participating. One day he approached Jerry. These two men represented some of the "old heads." Navy Lieutenant J. B. McKamey had been in prison nearly four months longer than Jerry; they each knew what the other had endured. Over the years they had lived all around each other yet never in the same cell.

"Tom," said J. B., "I'm going to teach you to play bridge."

"Are you any good?" Jerry looked steadily at the lanky pilot, who he knew had faced all the same trials and tribulations over the years that he had.

"You bet. I have master points," said J. B.

"What does that mean?" asked Jerry.

"It means I'm d— good," grinned J. B. and turned to rummage up a deck of cards.

And so began a most rewarding master-apprentice relationship. J. B., with patience and commitment, was determined to make his student a suitable partner for any bridge tournament someone in the Hanoi Hilton might want to organize. And as time went on, Jerry realized he enjoyed the game tremendously.

Not long after the lessons began, while J. B. was dealing out four hands—two dummies and one for each of them—they began talking about their individual shoot-down experiences. Jerry knew the Navy pilot had flown an A-1 Skyraider, or Spad, the same type of airplane that had accompanied him on helicopter rescue missions. These attack bombers carried a respectable amount of ordinance. What he hadn't heard, however, were the details of J. B.'s shoot-down and capture.

"Where were you bombing?" Jerry asked him.

"My targets were north of Vinh," he said.

Jerry suddenly looked up. "When was that, J. B.?"

"Well, I had flown in that general vicinity before, but I was shot down on June 2, 1965," answered J. B.

Jerry sat a moment. "You know what—I was based at NKP—and I believe I was the one launched to go pick you up. We were already airborne and got a call that you had been captured!" said Jerry.

"Sure wish you had been able to get to me sooner," J. B. said, chuckling.

"Me too. I'd have saved you a lot of trouble—or at least tried," said Jerry.

J. B. nodded in agreement. "See—teaching you to play

bridge is the least I can do for the rescue helicopter pilot they sent after me!"

The knowledge of their close encounter prior to captivity sealed their friendship. Now the master-point bridge player was more determined than ever to produce a star student. Together they won many tournaments at the Hanoi Hilton.

■ ■ ■

Jerry was working on his Spanish vocabulary for an upcoming "exam" when a guard came into the cellblock and directed him to the camp commandant's office.

Now what? Jerry thought. No POW ever knew for sure what would happen when guards escorted him somewhere.

The turnkey led him into a small room with a desk. On top lay a letter. As Jerry sat down, he saw something else besides the paper. He picked up two small photographs—the first images he had been allowed to see of his children since his capture six years before.

All he could do was stare at the people in the photos. He knew who they were, of course, but in another sense, he just simply didn't recognize them.

Tommy had just turned seven when he left for Thailand in April 1965. This young man was nearly thirteen, with hair below his ears, broadening shoulders. He looked like a line-backer. His face was full yet already showing signs of early puberty—not the boyish grinning child he had kissed good-bye in Alexandria, Louisiana.

But it was his little daughter who had changed the most. Lori was four years old when he had left—not much beyond toddling and still with thin, wispy hair. The young girl he looked at now was ten years old, with long, dark hair and a dimpled chin, beautiful beyond words. She looked like her mother.

He tried to imagine them speaking—to hear their voices saying "Daddy." Suddenly, the tears flowed.

Though he couldn't imagine why, the guards allowed him to take the pictures back to his cell, where he shared them with some of his cellmates. They all agreed how handsome the children were.

That evening as he lay on the floor, he stared at the pictures for a long time.

Thank you, God, for taking care of them. They have changed so much . . . do they remember me?

Jerry knew that of course Terry would keep his memory alive in their minds—he was not worried one bit about that. But would they *remember* him? He knew Tommy would have memories, but how many Lori had of him, he wasn't sure. She had been so little when he left. His kids had loved him before, and he had loved doing things with them . . . but that seemed like another life, another person.

Please get me home, God. Take care of them, God, until I return.

He placed the pictures under the thin, blue sweater that was rolled up beneath his head.

■　■　■

As 1971 dragged on, the "university" classes continued, accomplished without aid of pen, paper, textbooks, or dictionaries.

The POWs often mentioned how they wished they had reference books.

But there was one book above all others that many POWs ardently wished they possessed: a Bible. For many years, POWs held in North Vietnam weren't allowed to receive packages from the States. Finally, however, this prohibition was lifted, but boxes had always been opened, contents pilfered, and any Bibles confiscated.

Over the years, Jerry's wife attempted several times to send him a copy. Of course, he never received any of them. And once in captivity, one of his greatest regrets was not having taken time to memorize more Scripture during previous years of his life. He missed the Bible—he had no idea before prison just how intensely he would. In place of Bible verses, Jerry relied heavily on great hymns of the faith, which often echo Scripture in their words.

From the beginning of their imprisonment, men had whispered or tapped Scripture verses they knew by heart through the walls. When they couldn't remember a certain verse in a passage, they would improvise. When they were repatriated, many POWs said how amazing it was, the accuracy they maintained without realizing it. Scripture was their light in the darkness. And what faith men had in their hearts they shared, like Jerry when he led in Communion with the unseen man on the other side of the wall at the Zoo many years before.

But many POWs longed for a Bible. The SRO in Jerry's cellblock continually petitioned the camp commander to allow them to have one. And if any of the men were called in for a "quiz," they also would ask. Jerry always repeated the request for a Bible every time he endured an indoctrination session.

Finally, the camp commandant at Unity told Big Room 3 he would allow one POW to come into the quiz room and read a Bible. When that message came back to the cells, the prisoners called a meeting.

"I think we should select one person to go in and ask to copy verses—someone who already has a fair knowledge of Scripture . . . and can write fast," said Jerry. The other men agreed, and Jim Ray, one of the seasoned POWs, was selected. Jim was familiar with several different Bible translations, and everyone thought that might be beneficial.

In addition, Jim had been a soloist at his home church in the States, often singing hymns based on Scripture. During the first church service at Camp Unity, when Jerry heard him sing, he immediately recognized the voice: the one that had sung "O Holy Night" over camp loudspeakers during that bleak Christmas at Briarpatch.

So the men began to pool what Bible verses they already knew by heart. Out of nearly fifty men in Big Room 3, it was surprising how many they could remember collectively. Sometimes, if someone knew only part of a psalm or passage, someone else could fill in what he didn't remember. Jerry knew the familiar verses children usually memorize growing up in Sunday school, but he wished he knew more. He promised himself he would memorize more Bible verses once he got home.

Men in Big Room 3 who were participating in the project— and that was nearly everyone—now began to decide which verses or passages they wanted Jim to copy. As they discussed the project, they decided on a few favorites for reading and meditating. Jerry agreed with the others—the Sermon on the

Mount was definitely a key passage they wanted, as well as chapter 13 of 1 Corinthians.

The day came when Jim was allowed to go to the interrogation room where the camp commandant awaited. As he entered, there was a small Bible lying on the table with paper and pencil. He sat down and turned to Matthew chapter 5 to begin copying the Sermon on the Mount. The Bible was a tattered-looking copy of the King James Version.

The camp commandant started talking. "I give you one hour. No more. You copy but must do here . . ." As he talked, he placed his elbow on the page of the Bible Jim was trying to record. He sat there for nearly fifteen minutes of Jim's hour, covering the Scripture passage Jim had selected.

When he finally sat back in his chair, Jim copied as fast as he could. At the hour's end, he folded the piece of paper and was led back to the cell.

"Here it is," said Jim.

Jerry and others immediately asked him to read out loud what he had copied. They sat around on the floor or on the sleeping platform to listen. It was the first reading of Scripture Jerry had heard in six years.

"Blessed are the poor in spirit: for theirs is the kingdom of heaven. Blessed are they that mourn: for they shall be comforted. Blessed are the meek: for they shall inherit the earth."

A hush fell over the men.

"Blessed are they which do hunger and thirst after righteousness: for they shall be filled. Blessed are the merciful: for they shall obtain mercy. Blessed are the pure in heart: for they shall see God."

Jim's voice was the only sound in Big Room 3.

"Blessed are the peacemakers: for they shall be called the children of God. Blessed are they which are persecuted for righteousness' sake: for theirs is the kingdom of heaven."

Finally, Jim reached the end of the Beatitudes. Unseen light permeated the room.

"Blessed are ye, when men shall revile you, and persecute you, and shall say all manner of evil against you falsely, for my sake. Rejoice, and be exceeding glad: for great is your reward in heaven: for so persecuted they the prophets which were before you."

Jerry thought the reading of Scripture that day had never sounded sweeter in his life.

After he finished reading, Jim passed out the verses to several of the men who wanted to continue to study them later that night. Jerry received the verses about how God's children are the light in the world. The POWs all agreed having Scripture they could hold in their hands was one of the greatest things that had happened since their imprisonment.

The next morning, however, as guards entered Big Room 3 inspecting for the usual contraband, they found the pieces of paper with English writing. Immediately they confiscated all of what Jim had copied and distributed among the POWs.

"We take papers! Give back now!" The guards were yelling and began sweeping aside blankets and clothing to locate all the pieces of paper.

"Wait," said Jerry. "You said we could do this."

"You must give back! No keep!" growled the guard.

Reluctantly, the men who held the precious pieces of paper with Scripture written on them gave up their bits of treasure.

Jim stepped forward. "But I can continue to copy. The camp commandant said I could."

"You can . . . but no keep. No keep!" The guards retrieved every bit of paper and rushed out of the room.

"Well," said Jerry, "we will just have to start memorizing whatever Jim copies. They can't take it away from us then."

So the next time Jim went in to the interrogator's room, he copied as fast as he could. He began with 1 Corinthians 13. He ended the hour by recopying parts of the Sermon on the Mount, since the men now thought they could piece most of those chapters together.

This time when he returned to Big Room 3, he tore the paper into sections and handed them out to as many POWs as wanted to participate—and most did. They spent the rest of the evening memorizing the verses on their pieces of paper.

Sure enough, shortly after breakfast, guards came in to inspect the cell again for contraband. They did find the papers with verses written on them, but this time, it didn't matter. The POWs handed them over without regret, because they held the verses in their hearts. The "living" Bible had been born.

Each week, the recorder had to return what he had copied the previous day. But the V quickly realized the spiritual lift the Bible verses seemed to be giving the men. This frightened the guards, especially the camp commandant. He only allowed about six one-hour recording sessions, then abruptly stopped the copying.

However, between what prisoners knew from memory collectively and what had been copied and memorized, they could recite the entire Sermon on the Mount, Romans 12, 1 Corinthians 13, many of the Psalms, and various other passages scattered throughout the Old and New Testaments.

Jerry treasured being able to learn more verses. And when

someone felt a need to hear a certain Scripture passage, there usually was someone who knew it, would be willing to recite it, and would help a fellow POW memorize it. As Jerry watched another POW exercising, he realized he could go to him and ask him to recite the verses he held in his heart. The prisoner found it so uplifting to think, for example, that "John 1:1-5" was doing push-ups over in the corner. The one Bible the POWs constructed was perhaps the greatest that exists—a truly "living" Bible. Jerry thanked God for it every night.

■   ■   ■

One evening, as he was drifting toward sleep on the concrete platform with its eighteen inches of sleeping space per man, Jerry began his usual talk with God. That week, a ferocious pink-eye epidemic had swept through his cellblock. All fifty men confined in Big Room 3 had contracted the disease except for him and one other person. Those affected suffered eyes badly swollen and struggled with severe pus and redness. The medics had nothing for it. Jerry had spent several days delivering wet rags to comfort men seeking a little relief from burning and itching.

God, please help my cellmates. Heal their eyes quickly. They need your touch.

Then, he reviewed the Spanish and French he had learned that day and his next speech for Toastmasters Club. As usual, his thoughts drifted to his family—he wondered if Terry had to help the children sometimes with homework. Did they like school? He prayed they did.

Before joining the Air Force, Jerry had completed two years

of college—only his finances had prevented him from continuing along that path. His entry into the Air Force, at first, was really because he needed secure employment. But he discovered he loved to fly and loved visiting other places. He had seen so many things most people never see as long as they live, and he had experienced things only written about in books.

As he reflected, he realized the extent of his desire for learning. He had always had an innate curiosity about things—history, mechanics, people. It seemed ironic that here in a prison, an oppressive place that constantly reminded him of his confinement, his mind was soaring. He was receiving a quality education.

CHAPTER 16

THE 4TH ALLIED POW WING

MAY 1972–FEBRUARY 12, 1973

AS THE US-VIETNAM PEACE TALKS continued to grind through the summer and fall of 1972, it appeared no one could agree on anything. Disputes over every part of the Paris Peace Accords threatened collapse of the process—representatives of governments attending the meetings argued for weeks simply on the shape of the negotiating table. It seemed as if the war would never end.

Meanwhile, POWs cocooned in Vietnam cells waited. Their last several months of captivity were some of the tensest they had faced, especially for those men known as the "old heads," the servicemen who had been prisoners from the beginning of the war.

In May 1972, Jerry and others at Camp Unity learned about

the possibility of yet another relocation from a Vietnamese A-1 pilot, code-named "Max," imprisoned with them. "Max" had overheard guards discussing an upcoming move of POWs, but the pilot had not been able to determine how many prisoners would be involved or where they would be taken.

One night a short time later, guards unlocked the door of Big Room 3 and briskly entered with their arms outstretched, making rolling motions with their hands. Jerry had seen that sign multiple times over the past seven years. It was time to move again.

As the POWs were marched out the door, Jerry counted sixteen trucks waiting, engines running. Then he saw guards bring out dozens more men from all over Camp Unity. He nudged the POW standing next to him. "I'll bet there are at least a couple hundred of us going," he muttered under his breath. It was obviously a relocation involving the largest number of POWs since he had been brought into the prison in 1965—a move of great magnitude.

Before guards loaded them into the large convoy, each man had his hands cuffed behind his back. About a dozen or so were loaded into the back of each truck, sitting anywhere they could on the flatbed. Canvas stretched over metal frames, concealing the prisoners from view. Before pulling out of Camp Unity, guards placed one open bucket for a toilet in the back of each truck.

The long convoy rumbled out of Hoa Lo Prison into the deserted, nighttime streets of downtown Hanoi. It moved slowly until it got to the city's outskirts, then picked up pace, traveling into the country. Before long, the trucks were speeding on dirt roads, obviously rushing to their destination.

Jerry strained to stay seated upright with his hands cuffed behind him. The convoy traveled all through the night, finally stopping just before dawn the next morning. He wasn't sure where they were—they sat in the trucks during daylight hours. Toward dusk, guards gave them a little water and bread.

As soon as it was dark, the convoy cranked up again and sped onward. Some POWs had a general sense they might be moving on a northward path because roads became steeper and bumpier, perhaps signifying the mountainous areas north of Hanoi.

"Where do you think they're taking us this time?" John Frederick, a burly Marine, whispered to Jerry.

"I've no idea, John," said Jerry. When the POWs in Big Room 3 at Camp Unity had just celebrated Frederick's forty-ninth birthday, it didn't stop the man who had been in the Marine Corps for nearly thirty years from demonstrating he still had what it took to be in the Corps. After they had sung "Happy Birthday," he dropped down and performed one hundred short-arm push-ups, barely winded afterward.

Jerry knew John from prison population lists he had memorized but had not lived with him until Camp Unity. The stalwart warrant officer quickly became one of his favorites. They both had endured the same amount of physical abuse and torture—John had been shot down just a couple of months after Jerry, in December 1965. They also had shared stories with each other about their children, though John's were older than Jerry's. Each man agreed missing their families was the hardest part of being a prisoner of war.

The trucks continued to race along, deep potholes and hairpin curves rendering use of their one small communal toilet bucket nearly impossible. Many were suffering from severe intestinal disorders, and shortly into the second night of the trip Jerry's kidneys shut down—he simply couldn't void. The pain was excruciating.

They traveled for three days, moving only at night and hiding under trees in the daytime. Roads were getting steeper and temperatures lowering, which indicated they were indeed climbing upward into a mountainous area. Although the POWs weren't sure where they were being transported, they realized this was no ordinary move. The unusual distance and large number of prisoners caused concern all around, if not outright alarm. For Jerry, it was by far the most nightmarish relocation he had endured during his entire time in North Vietnam.

At last they reached their destination. Jerry could barely rise when the convoy stopped. John Frederick helped him down from the truck, and Jerry managed to hobble to his cell. At last he was able to drink some water. Fortunately, within about twenty-four hours, his kidneys started functioning again.

During the next few days, the POWs learned they were only seven miles from the Chinese border and about a hundred miles due north of Hanoi. Their prison was a new maximum-security facility located in a small valley surrounded by desolate mountains. A high brick wall surrounded the front side of the prison, and a soaring karst blanketed and topped with barbed wire buffered the rear. Black paint, along with vines and branches, camouflaged the roofs. One airman said the only thing that kept it from being a dungeon was location—it wasn't underground.

Though the prison was newly constructed, Jerry found the dozen or so stone and concrete buildings even gloomier, colder, and damper than any facility in Hoa Lo. The unusually thick walls contained only narrow slits for windows. There was no electricity. Since high mountains surrounded the complex, total darkness engulfed the cells fourteen hours a day. POWs soon nicknamed this obscure place "Dogpatch."

Men were divided into groups of eight to twenty, filling the empty concrete rooms. The primary topic of conversation was why had they been moved so far out of Hanoi—did it indicate a positive omen or a dangerous situation? Not surprisingly, opinions varied widely as to what all of this might mean.

One of the reasons many thought the move possibly was a favorable sign was related to their individual shoot-down dates. These men represented roughly the first two hundred servicemen captured, beginning with Lieutenant Everett Alvarez Jr., the first prisoner taken captive (on August 5, 1964). Alvarez, a Navy fighter pilot, would become known affectionately as "the Old Man of the North." On the other hand, why had they been moved to such an isolated location in the first place?

Jerry was placed in a building with approximately three cells. During the day, the prisoners could commingle, but at night, fifteen or so men were locked into individual cells. John Frederick and Will Forby were both in the cell group with Jerry.

At night, he would sit in the pitch darkness of his remote prison, praying for strength and wondering what this latest move so far away from Hanoi might signify.

A few weeks after POWs occupied these cells, guards distributed outdated American magazines, though many sentences were blotted out. As Jerry thumbed through the pages, he thought of all he had missed during the past years—seven and a half now, counting the time he had been in Thailand before his shoot-down. The people in them looked so different from what he remembered. He wondered, as he often did, what his son, Tommy, looked like as a teenager, and what his little daughter, Lori, looked like. He missed them. But he missed Terry most of all.

Out of the blue, he found himself wondering what sort of hairstyle she wore now. The magazine pictures showed women with very large, bouffant styles, which some of the men in camp referred to as "bubble-tops," and many men in the States were pictured with very long hair. Double-knit suits sporting wide-bottomed pant legs looked odd for guys. On the other hand, the short, colorful miniskirts for women looked interesting. The younger shoot-downs expressed hope this particular style would still be in vogue if or when they ever returned home.

No sooner had someone framed a statement in that manner than silence followed. Jerry knew things would be different—*how* different was the question. The North Vietnamese guards never spared sharing with them information about the thousands of Americans who demonstrated, protested, and rioted concerning US involvement in the war.

Captors continued to repeat every negative and hateful pronouncement against them by their countrymen in the States. And they just as eagerly shared any sympathetic and pro-Communist statements—especially those from other Americans. In fact, over the years, POWs felt they could discern the ebb and flow of the severity of their torture relative to the amount of protests erupting in America.

At this point, however, the two-hundred-plus men just a stone's throw from the Chinese border had little way of knowing what was transpiring in Hanoi, much less the United States.

They might as well have been on another planet, confined as they were in Dogpatch.

Like being allowed magazines, several other aspects of Dogpatch actually seemed to be slight improvements over other camps where Jerry had been confined. The fifty-five guards adopted a "live and let live" attitude. Since daylight was shortened, prisoners were allowed to spend time in the hallways of their cells visiting. However, they were locked up again after dark, which was most of the time.

Food was minimally better here than in Hoa Lo, even though rice replaced bread. Later, they were given books, primarily Russian propaganda books translated into English.

Even with these slightly more favorable conditions, there was one major deficiency at Dogpatch that proved devastating. Due to colder and damper interiors, illnesses escalated. Though Hanoi meted out medical treatment sparingly, here in this remote location there was little, if any, available.

One day, Jerry noticed John Frederick had spent a couple of mornings not doing much more than just lying on his bunk. He decided to check on him.

"John, are you okay?" he asked.

"Oh yeah, I think so," said John. "Just feeling a little weak—that's all."

But Jerry worried. He knew it was not a good sign for someone as strong as John. He talked to a couple of others in the cell, including Will. "I think we ought to see if we can get the guards to do something," said Jerry. Will agreed.

The next morning when they were allowed into the hallway, a POW said to the turnkey, "Bao Cao, Bao Cao," the familiar call to speak to someone in authority.

A guard came who spoke limited English. They asked him to send a Bac Si, or medic, to check John. When the guard returned, he brought a medic, who gave John one aspirin.

Later that night, Jerry felt John's forehead. He was clammy. "Maybe that's a good sign, John. Maybe you've sweated off a fever. You will probably feel better in the morning."

John did feel somewhat better the next day but still was not his normal self. For nearly a month, this continued with his fever constantly spiking and breaking. Jerry and the other cellmates watched helplessly as the brawny Marine grew weaker and weaker with each passing day.

The next time a medic came to check on him, he ordered John removed from the communal cell to an isolated one. A few days later, POWs in another building saw a truck pull up to that same isolated cell at night, and they thought they saw a man being carried out on a stretcher.

Jerry asked the guards about John the next day. They simply answered, "In hospital. In Hanoi. Taking soup." He prayed for his friend who had served his country so valiantly for thirty years.

Each time after that, the guards always replied the same thing when the POWs asked about their friend. But John never returned to Dogpatch.

The situation devastated Jerry and the other POWs. They all had gained such an appreciation for this brave Marine who, at nearly fifty years old, had taken everything the V had thrown his way. Jerry continually prayed for his friend, for God to make him well and return him home to his family.

Fall eroded into winter at Dogpatch. It was cold and depressing, and Christmas was fast approaching—Jerry's eighth in captivity. In this remote facility, POWs lived together basically in the same groups they had been with for the past two years. Once again, Jerry was in charge of planning Sunday services for anyone who wanted to attend—and usually most men did.

One Monday morning during planning for the upcoming Sunday church call, Jerry approached a younger POW and asked him if he would give a devotional during their worship time. The airman declined, saying so many others were more qualified than he was. Jerry didn't pressure.

"Okay . . . maybe just think about it," he said, "and let me know."

A couple of days later, the young officer approached Jerry and said he would do it. Jerry had no idea what a powerful message they would hear.

When Sunday arrived, the other POWs began sitting down on their wooden bunks. In the informal setting, the young pilot stood up.

"Well," he said, "here goes." He fidgeted with his hands, obviously uncomfortable. "When Jerry came to me and asked if I would speak to you guys today at our Sunday service, I told him, 'Hey, I'm not a church person.' There are so many of you who could be doing such a better job of this than I can." He spoke softly, hesitantly.

"But after I thought about it, I went back to him and said okay—I'd do it." The other men were listening now, intently.

"I don't know much about the Bible—however, what I do know is what we've been through here in prison. We've been hungry. We've been beaten. We've been abused."

None of the men who sat before him needed to be reminded of their plight, but there was something profound about the retelling. The sound of the speaker's quiet voice going over the litany of abuses and hardships they all had endured brought the brutal reality of their situation to the forefront of their minds. They were prisoners of war in a hostile environment. They had endured everything the North Vietnamese had dished out.

"And here, so far away from our country, our families, our homes—we have nothing. Everything has been taken away from us," the young man said.

It was absolute fact: the men sitting before him had been stripped of all external possessions. Of material things, they had nothing to their names—nothing. Though some speculated the war might be drawing to a close, there was no solid information to confirm that. And the fact that the V had transported them to such a remote place caused many grave concern. Fresh on everyone's mind was John Frederick. They still didn't know what had happened to him.

"But in reality," he continued, "we each have many gifts—call them talents, if you want to—but we each have something that God has given us."

He stopped speaking for a moment and picked up one of their enameled tin plates stacked on a nearby bunk. Now, he came to the heart of his message, holding the empty container in his hands.

"Though we have nothing materially, we each possess something, a gift or talent within us—something we can give to God for him to use. As I pass this empty dish around, I want each of you to hold it for a moment. Whatever you have that you are willing for him to use, place it in the plate—whatever you are willing to give to God." He handed the plate to the first man sitting closest to him.

There was complete silence, just the subdued sounds of an

empty plate being passed from one man to the next. Each man held the plate for several seconds. Many could be heard stifling their emotions. Some wept openly.

As Jerry watched the powerful yet simple message being delivered by this inexperienced teacher, he thought about how he had asked God during that first year in prison to use him in these dark dungeons whenever possible. And God had done that many times over.

Now Jerry recognized God had used him once again. God was answering his prayer of seven years before. Yet one more time, he had become a conduit for God's light—this time through him to another POW and out again to others, a moment full of unspeakable purpose during his imprisonment.

Jerry was the last to touch the plate with its invisible contents. Only God knew its weight.

■　■　■

Back in Hanoi, when the other prisoners learned of the large number of men who had been moved out to an unknown destination, the leaders and senior officers discussed the situation. Some believed it was a sure indication that things had begun to progress with peace negotiations—they just didn't know in what direction. They were all convinced the Communists wanted to protect a cache of their prisoners in the event they were needed as bargaining chips.

Others thought it indicated a dire situation. They hashed over what would happen should the prison be overrun by locals in Hanoi. Many remembered the massive crowds and near-tragic results of the Hanoi March back in 1966. Others speculated the V might carry out mass executions of all POWs should the United States invade Hanoi. So many unknowns—the Communists could never be predicted.

Then, in mid-December, what began as another ordinary, monotonous day at Camp Unity in Hanoi quickly turned into the most unbelievable day they had experienced in prison. Long-silent air-raid sirens suddenly started to wail. Then, several detected a distant roar. It grew louder and louder until someone shouted, "Do you hear that?" They felt the ground begin to shake violently, and within moments plaster began falling all around them inside the cells. Squadrons of B-52s commenced bombing Hanoi on December 18, 1972.

"We knew we were supposed to dive under anything we could, but most men went to the windows and just cheered," remembers one POW. It had been years since any of them had heard the sound of airplanes overhead. Later, John McCain said it was the most spectacular show of air power he would ever see.

In his book, *When Hell Was in Session*, Admiral Jeremiah Denton describes the event:

> Our captors were stunned by the tremendous bombardment and as the B-52s continued the assault nightly, leading up to Christmas, the camp hierarchy began to lie low and play strictly by the rules with us. They began to defer to our senior officers and appeared badly frightened.
>
> The bombing stopped on Christmas Eve, and I prayed that the antiwar people would not deter Nixon from resuming the bombing after Christmas. I believe it was the most decisive moment of the war.

After the bombing began, there was a general sense that perhaps things really were winding down, that their days in Hanoi were limited. About 130 Americans were taken prisoner in 1972, a large portion in December. Fifteen of the B-52s were shot down, the survivors brought into the prison at Hanoi.

These new captives shared news of the status of the Paris peace talks and what was taking place back home, primarily political developments. The deliberations in Paris had stalled, and with intelligence reports of POWs being taken to a remote location near China, President Nixon had made the decision to begin bombing Hanoi and the surrounding region, focusing on military targets.

Most military experts then and military historians since believe it was in large part the renewed bombing that secured the successful release of the POWs. It explains how, as a group, those men who were incarcerated within the prison system of Hanoi would always regard Nixon as the one ultimately responsible for bringing them home.

■   ■   ■

Late in January 1973, Dogpatch guards loaded their two-hundred-plus prisoners into trucks, bouncing again over dirt roads descending back down from that remote mountainous area near the Chinese border. When they arrived at Camp Unity, others who had remained in Hanoi quickly updated them on all that had happened concerning the bombings during their absence. "I wish I could have seen it," said Jerry.

Yet he knew the V couldn't be trusted. The "old heads" who had been in captivity the longest had had their chains jerked too many times throughout the years to get excited before concrete evidence surfaced.

But even these seasoned POWs had to admit there were some noticeably positive signs. First, when the Dogpatch prisoners returned to Hoa Lo, the V kept POWs grouped together according to shoot-down dates, the accepted method of release once that time came. Second, the lights on guard towers and elsewhere around the camp were kept burning through the nights, signifying lack of concern by the North Vietnamese for continued air raids. Third, the airmen began receiving increased amounts of food: a half cup of reconstituted milk laced with sugar in the morning and extra bits of meat at night.

Some men reasoned the additional food might be an attempt to boost the health of those who looked undernourished. Also, the fewer men who needed to be carried out on stretchers the better in terms of public relations for the North Vietnamese. For the duration of the war, the captors had claimed that all prisoners had been treated according to the terms of the Geneva Conventions.

Still, no one ever verbalized, "You are going home." One day, however, the Hoa Lo camp commandant himself allowed something to happen that seemed to point to an ever-closer release date. After so many years, the scene symbolized the pride of those who remained, even though captivity had suppressed their true identity.

Jerry found the event unfolding before his eyes as surreal as anything he had witnessed in the seven and a half years since his shoot-down and capture. Each man there that day probably felt the same, because in later years accounts would vary widely as to details.

Regardless of specifics, nearly four hundred POWs were allowed to gather together outside in the dirt courtyard of the prison—and to muster in parade formation, senior officers at the front with Vietnamese guards standing by, just observing. It certainly did seem to indicate a sudden, extraordinary change in attitude on the part of their North Vietnamese jailers.

Hardly anyone, however, showed overt emotions. This was partly due to leadership's instructions to maintain dignity and discipline, partly due to most being completely drained of physical and emotional strength. So as a group, they stood motionless. One POW remarked later, "We were hardly breathing as we formed ranks."

As he looked forward, Jerry watched the camp commandant begin to read a document he said pertained to a future event. It seemed to imply an end to military activities and alluded to the POWs' "release from prison," but there was no specific date as to when that would take place. Communist propaganda, as always, laced the message.

If Jerry had felt the chill of that January morning in 1973, he no longer noticed. *Could I really be hearing this correctly?* he wondered, but he kept his eyes trained forward. There was no movement from the few hundred men who were standing together in formation.

Colonel Risner, as SRO, was standing in the front of all the POWs at Camp Unity. He also was looking straight ahead as the camp commandant continued to read.

The document did say that if release happened, it would be done in increments of approximately 120 in order of shoot-down date, with sick and wounded going out first. The camp commandant—most POWs remembered him as the one they called "Dog"—then advised them to show "good attitude to end," the old admonishment, though no one really knew if it would be the last time they heard it or not. Their thin, gaunt faces remained passive, looking straight ahead, in group formation, dressed in their tattered, soiled prison clothes.

Are they still jerking us around? Jerry wondered.

But when the camp commandant finished reading, he turned to leave. At that moment the SRO startled everyone. Jerry stood mesmerized.

Colonel Risner, at the head of the formation, did a sharp about-face, his military bearing displayed with unapologetic pride. Though he was still dressed in ragged prison garb, some would say he never looked more dignified.

"Fourth Allied POW Wing, atten-hut!" Risner barked out the command, and four hundred servicemen immediately snapped to attention. One POW recalled, "The thud of eight hundred rubber-tire sandals coming together smartly was awesome."

In all his career, Jerry had never come to attention with such great delight. The name itself, "4th Allied POW Wing," had evolved as the SROs in Camp Unity sought to emphasize their military organization: "4th" stood for the number of wars the United States had been involved in during the century, and "allied" referred to the inclusion of Thai and Vietnamese POWs captured. Elation filled Jerry at being able, after seven and a half years, to express that which defined him, his commitment to the Air Force and his country. *We are a military formation even if we're wearing pajamas,* he thought to himself.

Every squadron commander immediately returned the SRO's salute and in turn signaled their units with a "Squadron, dis . . . missed." The undeniable expressions of pride in their military organization representing their country, which for so many years had been submersed in darkness—at times had endured even torture to protect—were witnessed now in the light of day for all to see.

Jerry was as honored to be a part of their group on that occasion as he had ever been. It felt good to be in formation and to be able to display the outward signs of allegiance and training. They all stood a little taller on that day.

When they reentered the cellblock from the courtyard, many POWs broke down into tears, others laughed quietly, but many met the day with continued subdued emotions as if lost in their own thoughts. No matter the visible reactions, it was overwhelming for everyone. These were sights and sounds of a day burned into their memories forever.

Jerry would never forget the image of Risner calling them to attention. He would never forget hearing the sounds of words so closely associated with their military bearing and the sound of heels clicking together in response, men acting in one accord.

During the next few days in February 1973, a flurry of activity seemed to suggest that this, at last, was the real deal—though many still remained reserved. Those who had been there the longest said they weren't ready to "party it up" quite yet. As Jerry said to a nodding Will Forby, "We'll believe it when we see it."

Up to this point, no Vietnamese official had actually verbalized the prisoners would be released.

The captors began what they were calling "exit interviews" beginning with the first group according to shoot-down dates, earliest first. Senior leaders stressed the necessity of avoiding both confrontation on one end of the scale and fraternization on the other. This was not the time to do or say anything that might instigate problems.

One of the issues that arose at the last minute was what to dress in, if and when they left the prisons. Everyone assumed journalists from all over the world would be there, recording the event. And both sides, North Vietnamese and Americans, had their own ideas of what they would wear out of the prison.

The captors wished to have the POWs look well-dressed for propaganda, as if they had been on vacation, and suggested brightly colored sweaters with dress suits. The prison population preferred to walk out in the ragged, dirty clothes representative of their abysmal environment—cruel conditions that had been enforced by the Communist regime from day one. The V would not allow them to leave in their tattered clothes. The POWs were not about to dress as if they had been on holiday.

The agreed-upon choice was a compromise: black shoes, dark trousers, and a lightweight gray jacket with a zipper. These were issued to the first 120 men who had been shot down. Guards then took these men, about six at a time, on February 11, 1973, to a section of Heartbreak Hotel, ironically where most of them had "checked in" when they were captured initially.

The POWs were also given a small black duffel in which to carry any personal items. Many men brought home their tin drinking cups, one of them remarking he had used it so long that it was as close to him as his baby cup had been.

Jerry went to the area to pick up his clothes, then over to a place where the V were giving haircuts. It was here he saw for the first time since his captivity the pararescue crewman from his H-43 helicopter that had been shot down. Neil Black had been incarcerated over the years in locations different from

Jerry. Sometimes they may have been only a few dozen yards away from one another but did not cross paths.

The two crewmen from Jerry's helicopter who were captured when he was on September 20, 1965—Black and Bill Robinson—became the longest-held enlisted servicemen in the history of the United States. Neil looked about the same; Jerry wondered if he did.

Once he got back to his cell, he and the other POWs were like little children trying on their new clothes. It was the first time in seven and a half years he had zipped a zipper or tied a shoelace.

That night, as Jerry prayed before sleep overtook him, uncertainty remained as to what might unfold over the next few days.

God, will this be my last night in captivity, or will something go wrong and turn the whole thing into a fiasco? Please, God, be with us tomorrow. Let this succeed. Please, get us home. Whatever the plans are, let everything go smoothly, keep us safe . . .

He recalled how he felt that very first night in captivity seven and a half years before as he tried to sleep and kept jerking awake: he was anxious and dead tired, all at once. He felt the same way now. All the signs looked good, but there was no way to know for certain whether they could trust the V, even at this juncture.

God, you have been with me all along. It hasn't been easy. I am so ready to get out of here and go home. Please, let everything progress smoothly tomorrow.

Jerry tossed and turned all night. He still had heard no North Vietnamese official actually voice that POWs would be released the next day.

. . .

As the men in their cells in Hanoi tried to sleep, they had no way of knowing for certain what was transpiring on their behalf elsewhere in the world. In the predawn darkness of February 12, 1973, four C-141 Starlifter crews, ready to take off, received an alert of bad weather over Hanoi, delaying their departure from Clark AFB, Philippines, for nearly two hours. It created tension all up and down the chain of command.

Concerned that any delay might jeopardize their mission—not just significant in humanitarian terms but of historic military importance—as soon as a slight break occurred, the planes were ordered into the air. Three would fly on ahead to Hanoi, while one circled at Da Nang, South Vietnam, as backup in case unexpected problems with the others occurred.

As the C-141s came into Hanoi airspace, the overcast presented a six-hundred-foot ceiling, the bare minimum needed to land the aircraft. Not knowing for certain the condition of the six-thousand-foot runway at Gia Lam Airport, the first plane began its descent and broke out from under the thick fog cover with barely enough clearance above the runway for landing.

Once the first crew saw the condition of the runway, that most of the holes created during bombing raids had been patched over, word was sent there was enough room for the second plane to land. However, in the delay of messages being communicated back and forth from 22nd Air Force at Travis AFB in California, the second plane was told to pull up and circle around, since there remained a question of suitable landing space on the runways.

At this point the North Vietnamese became furious and

began yelling for the second plane not to circle but to land. But it was too late. Due to the short runway, once the second C-141 was told to pull up and circle around, they had no choice but to continue on that course.

The incident, under any other circumstances, would have been a mere blip in the overall day. But tensions were high. No one knew for sure exactly what might transpire. Fortunately, the second C-141 circled around and landed shortly thereafter, avoiding any further issues for the present, while the third C-141 continued to circle. Now the crews, military officials, nurses and medical teams, escort officers, and State Department personnel sat on the runway of Gia Lam Airport, Hanoi, North Vietnam, waiting.

CHAPTER 17

FEET WET

FEBRUARY 12–16, 1973

JERRY AWOKE EARLY on February 12, 1973, as if he had never been asleep. For many minutes, he lay immobile, staring upward at cracked places in the ceiling. Somebody coughed next to him, and he realized men around him were awake but moving in slow motion.

Most appeared more dazed than alert: deep circles under everyone's eyes, dry mouths, gaunt faces, lifeless expressions. No one said much as they quietly climbed off their concrete sleeping platform. How could any of them know for sure what the next few hours might bring?

God, is today the day this nightmare ends? Please, God, make it so.

Jerry continued to pray as he moved to get up. The captive

looked down at the black satchel that held his new change of clothes.

Thoughts drifted in and out of his mind. As the POWs waited in their cellblocks, small groups formed here and there, talking quietly. Jerry looked around for Will Forby. "Well, what do you think?" Jerry asked.

Will shrugged his shoulders slightly. "Hard to say" was his cautious reply.

No sooner had the two cellmates exchanged these words than the cell door swung wide open and several guards entered. They made the familiar chopping motion at the wrists for POWs to put on their long shirts. This time, however, it wasn't prison pajamas but the new clothes they had received the day before. Many men found their hands trembling as they tried to button shirts and pull on trousers.

When they were dressed, guards motioned for everyone to exit into the courtyard. Several dilapidated buses were waiting for them. The POWs slowly assembled two by two in the courtyard and began to load up. No one said a word, and the guards didn't indicate where they were taking the POWs.

Jerry crossed over the threshold of the cellblock door, realizing it might be for the last time. He still was not allowing himself to think about freedom yet.

The several seriously ill POWs, a few on stretchers, were loaded before anyone else, so Jerry went out on the second bus—he was number 30 to be captured among nearly 600 POWs. He and Will sat together. The buses carried 116 men in the order of their capture, supposedly the first wave of POWs to be released. The remaining POWs were scheduled to be released at intervals over the following two months.

The buses slowly made their way out of the courtyard of Hoa Lo Prison, the Hanoi Hilton, and into the streets of downtown Hanoi. Jerry looked at the front of the prison—a different perspective from any he had had in seven and a half years.

The ride to Gia Lam Airport was somber. Oddly, many Vietnamese people lined streets to watch as the buses passed by, and some even waved. It felt surreal—as if the POWs were on a tour riding slowly through the streets. They were seeing Hanoi for the first time. The men talked very little, if at all, and then only just a word or two in low tones. When they arrived at the airport, they exited their bus quietly, cautiously. There was no high-fiving or cheering; everyone remained composed.

Jerry prayed frantically. *Oh, God . . . they have brought us to the airport. Can it be true? Can this be the day? Is our freedom at hand? It has been 2,703 days, Lord, since I was captured. Please, God, let it be. Let nothing go wrong . . .*

Once at the airport, the bus stopped a little distance away from the edge of several buildings forming the main terminal. From their vantage point, however, the POWs could not see the runways.

After disembarking the buses, men carefully formed up again, two abreast, and began to march quietly through the large crowd of journalists, photographers, military personnel, and citizens who had come to see them. Hundreds if not thousands lined the streets.

As they approached the other side of the airport building, the American captives could see a desk under a large tent where various Vietnamese military personnel were seated.

But it was the sight on the tarmac that caused Jerry's heart to jump to his throat. He breathed in quickly.

Like gigantic, resting beasts ready to spring to life were two of the most beautiful "birds" Jerry had ever seen—C-141 Starlifters. These planes had been introduced into the line after he was captured: he had never seen one before. The cargo planes were massive, with broad wingspans sleek and swept back and "United States Air Force" painted in bold, bright letters across their gleaming, white sides. Also painted on the planes' bodies were red crosses, international symbols for medic transportation. These C-141s would become known collectively as the Hanoi Taxi.

Now, many American military officers dressed in clean, crisp uniforms emerged and walked briskly toward the tents. With them, military escorts in flight suits displaying bright white ascots highlighted by embroidered POW emblems disembarked and headed toward the tents. Every bit of brass and the metal insignias on hats, shoulders, and buttons shined as they moved quietly and purposefully toward the POWs. The Americans looked otherworldly. Jerry was having a hard time keeping his emotions in check.

As POWs stood somber in formation, the Americans sent to participate in the repatriation process, called Operation Homecoming, were equally impressed with what they saw. Dr. Roger Shields from the Office of the Assistant Secretary of Defense for International Security Affairs, who led the task force in charge of planning and coordinating the prisoner release, said later he wished every American back home could have seen their servicemen that morning. Shields himself often said afterward that he had never been so proud to be an American as he was on that day.

The POWs waited for nearly two hours, continuing to stand

quietly in rows of two abreast. Jerry looked around at the large group of Vietnamese, military and civilian alike, gathered there. He saw nearly every one of the old foes, men who for 2,703 days of captivity had controlled his fate. Frenchy, Rat, Bug, Mouse, Gap, and many others—they were all present.

Yet the prisoners of war remained subdued and composed, their finest military bearing quietly on display. Jerry felt the most elation he had ever felt in his life internally yet remained completely controlled outwardly.

Jerry looked over at Will Forby, standing next to him. He had done his best trying to rescue this downed fighter pilot out of the jungles of North Vietnam on September 20, 1965. That was the start of their captivity, both men united by the same catastrophic events. During their lengthy imprisonment, he had told Will hundreds of times he wished he could have rescued him successfully—they had survived so much together. *God, thank you for this man and his friendship over the years. Let us return to freedom together, this very day. Let it happen now, what I could not accomplish seven and a half years ago when I tried to rescue him. Please, God, let today be the day.*

They had been standing a long time—Jerry felt numb. Finally, one of the North Vietnamese camp commandants began calling out each name, one at a time. When each POW's name was called, he would approach the desk to be greeted by a senior American military officer, then officially turned over to his escort officer, repatriated at last.

It was Jerry's turn. When he heard his name, he marched confidently to the desk where an Air Force colonel stood waiting.

Jerry stopped and saluted. "Thomas J. Curtis reporting for duty, sir," he said.

Behind him was Will Forby. The two men together, with an escort officer between them, walked toward the waiting airplane. The commitment to duty and honor was completed: Jerry accompanied to freedom the man he had been sent to rescue nearly eight years before.

The C-141 Starlifter sat on the runway, its enormous back ramp down, revealing the cavernous interior. Up Jerry walked, greeted by Air Force nurses who offered him refreshments—coffee, tea, Coke.

Coke, he thought to himself. *I'll bet they even serve it with ice!* He and Will walked up to the front of the airplane and sat down next to each other. Neither did much talking—they still had a "wait and see" attitude. As the other men began to settle into seats arranged in rows, six across with an aisle down the middle, they were given a sampling of US newspapers to read.

Slowly, all forty POWs in Jerry's group were on board, and the back ramp closed shut. It was eerily quiet, some noise and movement but mostly these "old heads" remained apprehensive. They had been held in the grip of a Communist country for way too long—and technically they were still. The enormous cargo plane gradually rotated in order to point its nose in the direction of takeoff. The aircraft commander then began to ease the multiengine aircraft down the runway, rolling slowly at first. Though a plane's cabin might be windowless, pilots recognize the sound and feel of various stages of an airplane on its way to slipping gravity. They sat waiting, listening instinctively.

Now came the moment all 116 fliers and other servicemen who were being released had longed to hear: the roar of four

21,000-pounds-force thrust, turbofan engines revving up. Put simply, raw power unleashed. Next, the distinctive lunge forward, then faster, faster, faster, and . . . airborne.

When these pilots who had been POWs for so long were airborne, there was a round of cheers and shouts. But even then, a blanket of guarded optimism remained over this particular group who had the deepest knowledge of their captors.

They asked one of the escort officers to go up to the cockpit to announce when they were "feet wet"—in other words, to let them know over the intercom when they were actually out of North Vietnam airspace and over international waters. Even now, they still did not trust the intentions of those who had held them in hell's grasp for seven years, some longer. These men wanted confirmation.

Finally, the aircraft commander came on the intercom and announced the most significant words of the day: "To all of you: feet wet." They were now over the Gulf of Tonkin and headed toward freedom. Though the heavy, thick door separating the cockpit from the cargo area of the C-141 was shut tight, able to muffle almost any noise, there arose such cries and shouts that the entire cockpit filled up with the passengers' exultation. Men clapped and whooped and pumped their fists in the air. They screamed and yelled and whistled. The jubilation continued on and on, reaching an overpowering crescendo.

In the deafening roar of men celebrating their liberty, Jerry silently thanked God. Then he gave Will, sitting next to him on the plane, a quick nudge with his elbow. His blue eyes brimmed with tears, yet he was grinning from ear to ear.

"See, Will," he said, "I told you if you stuck with me, I'd get you home."

■   ■   ■

The flight from Hanoi, North Vietnam, to Clark AFB in the Philippines took approximately three hours. Men talked, visited with each other, hugged the nurses and smelled their perfume, and smoked cigars and every pack of cigarettes the escort officers had brought along.

Jerry savored each moment, but for the majority of the flight, he remained in his seat, relishing the comfortable cushion. It was the first time he had sat on anything other than concrete and the small wooden stools used for interrogation and torture sessions for all these past years. He couldn't begin to fathom what a bed with a mattress and pillows would feel like.

He closed his eyes, but his mind continued to race. The day he had awaited for so long was finally a reality. It seemed like a dream.

Jerry chuckled to himself. *Some things will be easy to get accustomed to again*, he thought. Yet his mind continued to churn—so much still seemed a blur.

He tried to imagine talking to Terry, hearing her voice, listening to her words, but he couldn't make it materialize in his mind. For so long, he had thought about her and missed her. Now the day was soon approaching when he would see her again. He knew she wouldn't have changed in the important ways, but still, things would be different—he just didn't know how.

As the plane approached Clark AFB, the men seemed subdued once more, happy but lost in their thoughts. Since C-141s have no windows on either side, they couldn't see anything as they came in. But the second they began to walk down the steps, they couldn't believe their eyes.

Huge crowds of people were all over the airport, standing along the sides of the runways, along the fences, inside the terminal building, and lining the sidewalks all along the front of the terminal. As soon as they caught glimpses of the first POWs exiting the rear of the plane, they cheered wildly, waving flags, banners, signs, and posters.

Jerry was stunned—they all were, really. In his wildest dreams, he would never have imagined seeing this.

Television crews filmed the POWs as they disembarked the airplane and announced the names of each as they came down the ramp. This aired live back in the States, broadcasting in the early hours of the morning. Most military families stayed up all night watching.

Then as the freed POWs rode in buses to the base, crowds lined both sides of every street, clapping, shouting, cheering—men, women, children of all ages—welcoming them back. Jerry was certain every American from anywhere in the region must have been there.

When they arrived at the base hospital, a sea of people greeted them there, too. As they entered the hospital, they were met with the same reaction. Nurses, doctors, techs, and other hospital staff cheered, clapped, and whistled.

But as soon as Jerry entered the building, he caught sight of something that made his emotions soar. Every wall of every corridor was covered with children's artwork depicting the POWs and hundreds of simple "welcome home" messages. The walls were so covered with their artwork, he couldn't determine even what color they were painted. Everywhere he looked, all he could see was the unmistakable innocence of children's drawings and lettering.

He stopped in the middle of the hallway and could go no farther. Soon, he would be reunited with his own children. The full impact of that finally hit him.

After so many years of stoic resistance in the face of unrelenting horror, he had no self-control left. Jerry began to cry uncontrollably. He walked over to the wall covered with crayon art and leaned against it, sobbing into the crook of his arm.

■　■　■

Each returning man had been assigned an escort officer, someone who, after they arrived, would serve as an assistant for whatever these servicemen might need—errands, shopping, or whatever the case might be. These escort officers were chosen from among volunteers solicited by the Air Force. Major Fred Bergold, also an HH-43 rescue helicopter pilot who had spent a year in Pleiku, Vietnam, was stationed in Hawaii at the time. Several months before, when he had heard about the duty assignment, he volunteered and was selected.

Authorities in Washington knew the Paris Peace Accords had been signed, but nobody knew for sure when the North Vietnamese were actually going to release the POWs. Everything remained in a state of flux. So officials had all the escorts sent to Clark—they had been there for three weeks prior to the arrival of the POWs.

Each night at Clark AFB, a duty officer was assigned to monitor the status of events in Hanoi—if and when the C-141s would actually be alerted that they could leave the Philippines and head to North Vietnam. Fred happened to be the duty officer the night the alert came in. During the predawn hours, the

C-141s were airborne, headed to Hanoi to pick up and bring back the first wave of POWs to Clark.

As Fred looked over the list of names of those who would be aboard, he came across one that jumped out—Thomas J. Curtis, HH-43 pilot, shoot-down date 20 September 1965. *This man flew what I flew in Vietnam—that could have been me. That's who I want to escort,* he thought and began making plans to meet this rescue helicopter pilot in a few hours.

After the C-141s returned later that day and buses had taken the repatriated servicemen to the hospital, their assigned escorts arrived. Fred checked in and located Jerry.

"Lieutenant Colonel Tom Curtis?" he said, "I'm Major Fred Bergold, your escort officer. Welcome home, sir."

Jerry had been promoted from captain to major and then to lieutenant colonel while still in prison. It was the first time Jerry had heard anyone use his new rank when speaking to him.

"Well, it is good to meet you. But I tell you, Fred, I don't even know what a major is supposed to do, much less a lieutenant colonel!" The men shook hands warmly and walked to Jerry's first exam.

Doctors and nurses began tending to the group of men, most of whom had issues of one sort or another, some with serious physical problems. In planning for their arrival, doctors had made tags for them that read "Soft Diet," thinking after so many months and years of scant food to eat and of such poor quality, their bodies would need time to adjust to standard fare.

The near-riot that ensued caused doctors to change their minds. Orders were given for the kitchen staff to let them have whatever they wanted. Men began devouring huge amounts of everything—their bodies starving mainly for protein. As soon as he could, Jerry ordered a steak, fried eggs, and strawberry shortcake. It was the best meal he had ever had in his life.

All the escort officers had been briefed thoroughly on what they might encounter with the returning POWs. And since Fred had already served a tour of duty in Vietnam as a rescue helicopter pilot, he knew full well what had transpired in the prisons in Hanoi from reports and survival training.

At first, Fred kept the conversation fairly casual, but as he spent more time with Jerry, he thought what an exceptional person he was and what great mental shape this man was in to have endured what he knew Jerry had been through. And Jerry was immediately at ease talking with this particular pilot. They spoke the same language.

After a time, the conversation turned more serious.

"How did you manage all those years in prison?" Fred asked. "I know it was rough."

"Yes, it was, Fred," Jerry replied. "Really rough. But we held together. There were many, however, who didn't make it out." Jerry had been informed before they left Hanoi that John Frederick, the Marine he was with at Dogpatch, was listed by the North Vietnamese as having died in the hospital. Fifty-five men altogether were listed as having died in captivity in North Vietnam at this time.

"It was rough," Jerry repeated. "We took a lot of physical abuse, a lot of mental abuse. Those of us who went in at the beginning saw it all."

Fred listened as Jerry spoke softly, in a completely straightforward but quiet manner—no hyperbole or undue emotion.

"But I will tell you one thing, Fred . . . something we all

learned." Jerry paused and looked straight ahead. "Every man has a breaking point."

After their conversation, Fred accompanied Jerry to one of the rooms set aside for phone calls home. "Let me get your wife on the line for you, and then I'll turn it over," said Fred.

It was time for all the returnees to begin those long-anticipated phone calls home. Some were ecstatic; some were nervous; some found out they no longer had a wife to call—perhaps due to divorce or, in one or two instances, death. But everyone had some degree of anxiety. Each escort officer assigned to a POW initiated the phone call for the serviceman to ensure the connection went through. Once the wife or parent was on the line, he handed over the phone.

Jerry watched as Fred began to place the call to Alexandria, Louisiana. He felt like his mind was about to explode. He took several deep breaths while he heard Fred identifying himself to Terry and then saying, "Good, I have Tom here with me."

Jerry took the receiver. "Hello?"

"Jerry, how are you?" Terry said. "You look so good—I can't believe how good you look. We saw you on TV." Excitement and nervousness propelled her sentences rapidly forward.

Jerry choked down his emotions and couldn't say a word in reply, so Terry filled in the silence. She asked if Tommy was on the other line. "Tommy, are you there on the phone?"

"Yes, I am." The unmistakable, deepening voice of a teenage boy.

"Talk, Tommy—Jerry, you've just about got a grown son." His son had been only seven years old and was now almost fifteen.

No one said anything for a moment or two, and Jerry was

finally able to check his emotions. "I have some pictures you sent, and I cannot believe how big he is."

"How recent are those pictures?" asked Terry. Families had no idea what had been delivered to the prisoners and what had not.

Jerry told her he wasn't sure, maybe a year old. "I can tell how big he is though."

"How are you feeling?" Terry hardly knew what to say to her husband.

"I am fine, and I love all of you very much," said Jerry.

"Well, we love you, too. Do you know how much longer you will be at Clark?" said Terry.

"Probably another three days. The doctors will finish the medical check, and then we go to Travis. Where do you want to meet me?"

"We are supposed to meet you at Keesler in Biloxi," said Terry.

"Is Lori there?" Jerry's daughter had been four years old when he left for Thailand. Now she was nearly twelve.

"Tommy, get Lori on the phone," Terry called to her son. "Jerry—Mother, Daddy, and Fayrene are planning to meet us at Keesler too."

"Good," Jerry said.

"We are so anxious to see you. Have you had a big steak and baked potato?"

"Yes, I just had a delicious meal of steak and fried eggs and a little strawberry shortcake, and it was great."

Terry ran out of words.

"I can't tell you how much I have thought about you all these years," said Jerry. He struggled to keep his voice steady.

"Well, we have done the same. I know the Lord has been

with you just like with us, and I just know he is going to be with us now, and everything is going to be perfect." Terry felt in some ways like she was talking to a stranger.

"Well, let's hope so," said Jerry.

"I am sure it will. We just can't wait to get you here." Terry paused and both were silent for a few moments. "We are so excited," she added.

The conversation continued in this vein for some time, with pauses, tears, stumbles, mix-ups. They both had so much to say, yet they struggled to say it over the phone. They both noticed some subtle changes in the way the other sounded—deeper, more intense, different somehow. They were getting to know each other all over again.

"I'm so proud of you," said Jerry. "All of you—knowing that you were there, behind me all the way."

"Well, we have been—you are worth waiting for, needless to say—we just love you so much—" Terry sensed Jerry was crying. "We just can't wait to get to you—can't you rush them up a little bit?"

"They want to give us a good physical examination," he said, his voice catching just a bit. "I don't have anything wrong with me that I know of—nothing serious or major—maybe some dental work that needs to be done. A few other things—nothing serious," said Jerry.

Now it was Terry's turn to become quiet.

"I am not marked or scarred in any way," he said quietly.

"That's great," she said.

Choking back emotion once more, Jerry said, "Just as handsome as the day you married me."

"Oh, I won't be able to stand that then!" Terry paused a second. "You sound so good."

"Sweetheart," said Jerry, "there are others waiting to make calls too. But I think this will hold me until I can hold you and Tommy and Lori."

"We will be waiting right there—as soon as you get off that plane at Keesler. Just hurry up! Lori, do you want to tell your Dad anything real quick?"

Lori came to the phone, the little girl Jerry remembered with a child's voice. "Daddy," she said, her southern drawl pulling the word out slowly, "I got a dog."

"A dog?"

"Yes, sir," she said.

"What kind?" Jerry's voice was full of tenderness.

"A fox terrier, and her name is Precious." Unlike Tommy, who was seven when Jerry left for Thailand, Lori barely remembered the man she was talking to.

"Well, I have so much to catch up on, and I won't try to do it on the telephone. I love you so much. Tommy and Lori—thank you so much for taking good care of Mom for me," Jerry said.

"They did take good care of me. You'll be proud of them, Jerry, and we are proud of you, and we will be waiting for you."

"See you in about three days in Mississippi."

"All right, we will be there," said Terry.

"Bye, Lori. Bye, Tommy. Bye, Terry," Jerry's voice was giving way again. "I love you."

"I love you, too," Terry replied back.

"I'll talk to you later." Jerry couldn't wait for the moment when a million miles no longer separated him from his family.

Jerry hung up the telephone. Eight years apart is a long time.

But the awkwardness of the first phone call home was past, and even during the conversation, Jerry and Terry became more comfortable conversing with each other.

That night, Jerry reclined on a bed with a mattress, sheets, and pillows. He buried his face into clean, white linens—they smelled so fresh—and thanked God.

He suddenly realized something: the hospital mattress and blankets wonderfully buffered all the calluses that covered his ankles, sides of knees, and hips from nearly eight years of sleeping on concrete and wood. However, he learned the next morning that one or two of the group had slipped out and onto the floor during the night, unable to adjust to their soft beds. *Not me*, Jerry thought and laughed to himself. *Luxury feels great!*

The next day, Fred escorted Jerry to the clothing store on base to get fitted for a new uniform. Jerry looked in the mirror as the tailor began fitting his new blue coat and trousers. It felt so good to have a uniform on again. And since he had been promoted from captain to major to lieutenant colonel while still in prison, his new uniform would bear silver oak leaves, indicating his current rank—he never owned a set of gold major's leaves.

Then Jerry picked up some shirts and noticed the polyester. When he left for Thailand, none of the fabrics used in producing military clothing had any synthetics; all were subject to extreme wrinkling.

"Man, this polyester is fine stuff—no more ironing all the time," Jerry said to Fred.

"I know—you'll love it," said Fred. "You want to head on over to the BX?"

"Yes—that would be good," said Jerry. He had really missed wearing a watch in confinement, and at the base exchange, he quickly located a plain Seiko for thirty bucks. Socks, underwear, and black lace-ups rounded out his shopping basket.

A strong bond developed between these two men during their three days together at Clark AFB. Jerry was glad to learn Fred would also be the person to travel with him all the way to the States.

The group of POWs returning from Hanoi prisons filled their few days at Clark luxuriating in various ways. One man found a bathroom at the hospital with a large tub, went in, locked the door, and filled it with hot water to overflowing. Then he soaked for two hours. It would be the first of six baths he enjoyed—on his first night there. Others simply stood under hot showers for an hour or more at a time.

Once they were given the go-ahead to eat whatever they wanted, men who had been starving every day for years began ordering in abundance. The top item, even over steak, was eggs. One pilot ordered a dozen fried eggs and gulped them down within minutes. Others couldn't seem to get enough ice cream, returning to the buffet bar over and over to try every flavor available. Many wound up in bathrooms afterward—yet they all agreed it was worth it.

Initial physical examinations had commenced as soon as the former prisoners arrived. Numerous conditions would have to be addressed in the days and weeks to come, including bones that needed to be reset and gastrointestinal problems. Several returned POWs would require operations to correct problems brought on by torture, malnutrition, and grossly unsanitary living environments.

Almost all of them would be checked into base hospitals for treatment, convalescing, and debriefing. Jerry had beriberi, intestinal issues, and extensive dental work that needed to be addressed once he arrived at Keesler AFB in Biloxi, Mississippi.

After three days at Clark, the men of Operation Homecoming boarded another C-141 and headed toward the United States. For Jerry, it would mean retracing the route that had brought him to Thailand eight years earlier. During this flight, Jerry enjoyed being in the air again. He found a comfortable position and slept most of the way to their first stop.

The eleven-plus-hour flight carried them into Hickam Field in Honolulu, Hawaii, to refuel. Jerry got off the plane with his escort officer, where Fred's wife and two children waited to meet the returning hero at the airport.

"I'm on American soil again, Fred," Jerry said as they stepped off the plane. "I can't believe it. This feels great!"

As he walked down the stairs out of the airplane, another sea of people lined every available spot at the terminal, cheering, clapping, and waving flags and banners reading "Welcome Home POWs." The wild applause seemed to last forever.

Jerry accompanied Fred to meet his wife, Judy, and his two children who were waiting in the terminal. As Jerry reached down to say hello to Fred's young daughter, Bee, he asked her how old she was. She looked up at Jerry and said, "I'm seven and a half years old—that's how long you've been gone."

He stood quietly for a moment looking at Fred's little girl, then nodded. "Yes, it is—it's been a long time," he said, wondering again what his own daughter was going to look like.

For a couple of hours on the ground at Hickam, Jerry visited with Fred and his family. Bee had written him a letter:

Dear Lt. Col. Curtis,

Welcome back home. I am so glad you are back.
Thank you for serving our country.

Love, Bee

Jerry held it and couldn't speak for several minutes. He folded it and tucked it carefully in his pocket.

At last, the time had come to board the plane again, headed now for the mainland of America.

Jerry sat quietly on this part of the journey. He was suddenly overwhelmed with fatigue. Every limb of his body felt heavy, yet when he closed his eyes, his mind still raced. Jerry kept thanking God for his return.

The plane flew on to Travis AFB in California. Here, the layover was longer, since many of the men coming home from Hanoi needed immediate attention. The large hospital at Travis, a regional facility that had served as a medical hub all through the war, could offer the full range of services. As before, several hundred military personnel and their families, ecstatic about seeing the prisoners who were returning from Southeast Asia, formed lines around the airport and up and down streets.

When the enormous C-141 set down at Travis AFB, Jerry was in the continental United States again.

Jerry deplaned here on an errand. Fred asked if he could help him, and Jerry replied, "No, I'll just be a few minutes." He went into the terminal and sought the help of one of the other military escorts. After he finished his mission, Jerry climbed back aboard.

The C-141 flew then to Kelly AFB, Texas. On the way, sheer physical exhaustion once again caught up with Jerry. He slept all the way there. Yet again the traveling POWs were greeted by huge throngs of joyous crowds.

A few men got off here, but Jerry continued to Maxwell AFB in Montgomery, Alabama. Now, he could not even doze. He was near the end of his journey, and every nerve in his body was engaged.

The plane stopped briefly at Maxwell. Fred took the opportunity to call his wife, Judy. In an excited voice she told her husband what she had just received.

"Fred, the biggest bouquet of flowers I've ever seen arrived at our house a few minutes ago—it must be thirty inches tall and two feet wide—everything you can imagine: carnations, lilies, daisies, roses, birds-of-paradise—and they are from Lieutenant Colonel Curtis, thanking us for meeting him at the airport and thanking Bee for her letter."

Jerry's errand had been successful.

Now Jerry and one other returning pilot boarded a DC-9 and headed to Keesler AFB in Biloxi, Mississippi—to his wife, his son, and his daughter.

The past thirty hours had been a blur of flying, throngs of people cheering, sights and sounds of a different world—the world Jerry had left behind. To see women and children and not just men, with everyone dressed in colorful civilian clothing; to be able to walk around in any direction without a guard; to smell fresh air and cologne; to eat a candy bar and peanuts from a machine in an airport terminal—and all this just from flying on one trip—was a lot to take in.

Jerry felt no rough edges to his return. He suddenly realized how easy it was going to be to slip back into freedom, and he rejoiced in everything.

His mind was not yet ready, however, to begin unwinding the tapes of the past eight years. Some of that would occur during the next few days while he convalesced in a hospital at Keesler and began the formal debriefing process. These former prisoners who had been released first were all too aware of the hundreds remaining in Hanoi who were waiting to come home in the following weeks. They wanted to relay as much information as they could during debriefing that might help these others if possible. No one wanted to do or say something that might jeopardize the prisoners' well-being. Jerry also needed major dental work and attendance to a few other medical issues.

Now, during this last leg of his journey home, his thoughts once more turned to prayer.

Father, thank you again for taking care of us all these years, for providing for me and my family.

In a few minutes, the plane would land and he would be with them again. It almost felt as if it were the first time he had ever seen them.

Jerry thought about what the future might hold—there were so many things he wanted to do with his children: camping, school activities, and mainly just spending time with them. He was their father, and he couldn't wait to resume that role and try somehow to make up for lost time.

God, thank you for bringing Terry and me through these tough years. Help us put our family back together again.

The plane was coming in for its final approach. It landed and rolled to a stop, and attendants opened the doors. As usual, an enormous crowd had gathered to welcome the returning Vietnam POWs.

When Jerry emerged from the plane, he spotted Terry standing near the bottom of the steps. He descended, and within the next few moments he was holding his wife. Once he placed his arms around her, he didn't want to let go. He stood frozen for several seconds.

When he pulled back slightly, out of the corner of his eye, he saw a stout teenager with a young girl running as fast as they could toward them.

Could these be my children? The boy was so big, and the girl was a little lady—both such beautiful children.

When they reached him, Tommy said, "Dad?"

Jerry engulfed his son in his arms. Then still holding on to Tommy, he turned to Lori. "Sweetheart, I'm your daddy," he said. It was all Lori needed. She rushed into his arms as he leaned to meet her.

PART 3

AFTER PRISON

CHAPTER 18

HOME AT LAST

SHORTLY AFTER JERRY LANDED, the Curtis family, along with Terry's parents and Jerry's sister, were escorted to a small, one-bedroom suite with a kitchen and sitting area in guest housing on Keesler AFB. There they visited for a couple of hours, continuing to celebrate Jerry's return home with hugs and tears of joy.

But it was time for Terry's parents and Jerry's sister to leave with Tommy and Lori for their return to the couple's home in Alexandria. The grandparents planned to stay there with the children until Jerry completed his three-week convalescing at Keesler's regional hospital. Terry intended to stay with him, and then the couple would return home together.

Once everyone had embraced Jerry one last time, the family members left, and Jerry and Terry were alone in the small suite. They stood quietly looking at each other, the realization suddenly upon both of them that although they were husband and wife, they were also eight-year strangers.

Jerry broke the silence. "Are things still the same with us?" he asked with his usual penetrating gaze.

"Yes, of course," said Terry, attempting to sound as positive as possible. "Of course," she repeated but remained standing where she was.

"And you think we can work this out together after so long? It's been eight years," said Jerry. His voice was intense.

Terry nodded. "Yes, I want this to work too. And it will—we will make it work."

Jerry reached toward her and placed his hand under her chin. "I love you, Terry, so very much. And I'm so thankful you waited for me."

The woman who had occupied his thoughts more times than could be counted was now at last in his arms.

■ ▪ ▪

During Jerry's time at Keesler, medical and dental appointments, as well as complete debriefings, filled his days. Each morning Air Force intelligence officers recorded everything Jerry could remember about the situation in Hanoi. Since several hundred prisoners remained in North Vietnam, gathering as much data as possible was imperative. Names, shoot-down dates, and any information concerning any servicemen who may have been captured or lost in the theater of operation was of vital importance.

Then, each afternoon was consumed with medical exams and tests. But mostly, due to years of poor diet and hygiene, Jerry required time in the dentist's chair.

As he entered the dental office for the very first appointment, he shook hands with the dentist, an Air Force lieutenant colonel, who would be in charge of the extensive work he needed done.

"Sure hope this goes better than the last time I was in a dental chair," Jerry said to him while the dentist began pulling on his gloves and adjusting his light.

"How's that, sir?" the dentist asked.

"Well, the last time I was in a dental chair, it was just a crudely made wooden seat with a straight back and boards for arms in what looked like an empty concrete storage room," laughed Jerry.

"Oh, my," the dentist said, "that must have been in the prison in Hanoi. Tell me about it."

"I had broken a molar down to the gumline in 1967 on a piece of rock in my rice—it abscessed a couple of times a year after that. The pain was so bad, I had to sleep sitting up to let it drain. But when they thought our release might be imminent, the V began attempting to meet some of our physical needs. So one day last year, an armed guard took me to a small room I'd never seen before at the Hanoi Hilton. A medic who didn't speak a word of English—I'm not sure how much dental training he had—tried to extract what was left of the tooth," said Jerry, remembering back to the painful experience.

"He gave me what was supposed to be a shot of Novocain from the largest syringe I've ever seen, but it never deadened the area around my tooth," Jerry said. The dentist shook his head.

"Then," continued the patient, "he couldn't get any leverage on it. Time and again, he would try to get the instrument around it to extract it—each time he pulled, it felt like those roots were attached to my privates!" Jerry could laugh about it now.

"Oh, no!" said the dentist, "What happened—was he finally able to remove it?"

"Well, each time he yanked, I bolted upward in the chair—he knew I was miserable. He would take the syringe and give me another shot. I truly believe he was trying his very best to help me—and to keep from hurting me. But something was wrong with the Novocain—it just wasn't effective. Finally, he turned to the guard and said something. The guard left, and in a few minutes he came back with four bricks."

The dentist's eyes widened. "What on earth did he do with the bricks?"

"That is what I was thinking—don't tell me this guy is going to try to knock it out with a brick!" Jerry continued. "But he stacked the bricks beside that wooden chair so he could be taller and get more leverage on the tooth. He sliced open the gum and finally was able to dig down enough to get a grip on the roots. For about a month afterward, it continually sloughed off pieces of bone."

"Well, sir, why don't you lean back, and let's see if we can make this visit a little more pleasant," the Air Force dentist said with a laugh. He injected Jerry with enough anesthesia to deaden nearly his whole mouth.

Jerry lay back in the comfortable dental chair and fell sound asleep.

Repairing what had been done on that occasion, plus other deterioration due to lack of oral hygiene, kept the dentists busy nearly every afternoon the entire time Jerry remained at Keesler. Other issues concerned beriberi in his feet—which, once established, is primarily controlled with medication—and episodes he had experienced in prison with rapid heartbeats.

In late 1967, Jerry had noticed the onset of an irregular, racing pulse. He first became aware of it during winter months when prisoners often were cold soaked from lack of proper clothing. During this time, they also were experiencing additional stress brought about by worsening prison conditions and the trauma of renewed torture. While incarcerated, Jerry controlled his accelerated heartbeat with isometrics. Usually, this practice helped to bring his pulse back into rhythm, but often he just had to wait it out.

Yet Jerry felt extremely fortunate. Many POWs returned needing operations or rebreaking of bones that were set incorrectly (or never set at all), and several had permanently restricted range of motion in arms and legs from torture sessions.

While Jerry was busy with these tasks, Terry spent her time mainly taking long walks down by the Gulf. She could hardly believe Jerry was back. Terry could still vividly remember the afternoon she was told about Jerry's shoot-down. Notification arrived around 6:00 p.m. The doorbell rang, and when she answered, there stood a group of men in uniform on her front porch: a chaplain, a doctor, and two other servicemen from the detachment Jerry had been in. For a few minutes, no one spoke, and Terry invited them in. At first she hadn't suspected anything, despite that, as any military wife or mother knows, when people are standing on the doorstep in uniform, they usually are bearers of bad news.

They had informed her that Jerry's helicopter had been shot down and that he was listed as missing in action. That was all the information they had—he was just missing.

Terry knew her husband's mission in Southeast Asia entailed flying rescue helicopters for the purpose of extracting downed pilots. And she knew he had completed several successful missions previously, but not this time.

Almost as soon as she received this notification, her home filled with people—neighbors and church friends came over, family members drove in from Houston. Immediately, she was surrounded with love and prayers.

Terry remembered how those who supported her probably secretly thought Jerry had been killed, that he would not be coming home. Many people brought food, just as so many churches in the South do when there is a death in the family. But she never took this as a death message. She always knew there was hope. And now Jerry was back.

By late afternoon each day, they both looked forward to spending time together. He told her about his time in prison, and she related what life was like back in the States.

She told Jerry how, six months after he was shot down, she had received a phone call around 1:30 in the morning. It was from the mother of airman Bill Robinson, who had called with greetings from her son. Terry immediately knew there had to have been communication between Bill and Jerry—and that renewed her hope that Jerry was alive. She and her friends believed it was an answer to prayer.

A year later, when Jerry's status changed from missing in action to prisoner of war, there were three other women living in Alexandria whose husbands were also in Vietnam: one husband was a prisoner also; the other two were missing in action and, in fact, did not come home.

Terry and these three other women had formed a support

group for one another. They made trips to Washington, DC, to talk with whomever they could about the POW/MIA situation; they promoted letter-writing campaigns and collected signatures petitioning the North Vietnamese for better treatment of the men; they sold bumper stickers to remind people not to forget about their servicemen in Vietnam. Some women rented billboards to serve as a visible reminder for people in the USA of military servicemen in captivity.

But the biggest—and most successful—project had revolved around the national bracelet campaign. Wives and family members sold metal bracelets engraved with the names of a serviceman who was either a known POW or MIA. People were asked to choose someone they knew, or even someone they didn't know, in order to honor them. They were to wear the bracelets until either the men returned or they found out they were not coming home.

Terry had been so grateful to the people who had worn those bracelets and had prayed for the men. She attributed Jerry's homecoming to the prayers on his behalf.

Each day at Keesler that Jerry and Terry spent catching up was a blessing.

However, on the twenty-first of February, Jerry got dressed in his uniform and told personnel he was leaving and would be back in a couple of days. "I've missed seven of my son's birthdays, and I don't plan to miss another."

Jerry and Terry drove to Alexandria, Louisiana, to the house he had lived in eight years earlier. When they entered the neighborhood, Jerry saw sights he had thought about many times during the past years, but things looked so different. The houses had aged, the landscaping matured. Bushes and shrubs were now fully grown. Trees that had been nose high when he left towered over rooflines. He couldn't believe how tall they were.

When the couple turned down their street, Jerry was amazed by yet another incredible sight. Nearly every house celebrated the return of their friend and neighbor with homemade signs and banners, all welcoming back the wartime hero.

As they pulled up in front of their house, Tommy, Lori, Terry's parents, and Jerry's sister Fayrene waited outside for them. After another round of hugs and kisses, he entered through the front door. He was finally home.

The following day, the family celebrated Tommy's fifteenth birthday with presents and a feast of homemade cake and ice cream. For the time being, the couple decided to limit this visit to family only, rather than inviting friends and neighbors. Since Jerry had to return to Keesler in two days for more medical and dental checkups and continued debriefings, it allowed a quiet visit together. None of them could stop hugging their returned husband, father, brother, and son-in-law.

But the town of Alexandria and his church family made it clear that upon his permanent return in fourteen days, they planned to honor him properly with a parade and receptions.

And indeed they did. After his final days at Keesler AFB, Jerry went home to stay. Shortly afterward, a citywide parade with local high school marching bands, color guards, and other parade participants strutted before three-thousand-plus people crowded along streets and sidewalks just to catch a glimpse of the returning POW.

Jerry and his family rode in an open car, finally stopping in front of the review stand. After the mayor publicly welcomed the Curtises, the lieutenant colonel stood to address the hushed crowd.

"I just want to thank all of you for your thoughts and prayers while I was gone. It means so much to see all of you here today. God bless you, and God bless America."

The next day Jerry's church hosted a reception and, to Jerry's complete surprise, unveiled a project planned and executed quickly once his release had been assured: a flagpole on the church grounds with a large bronze plaque dedicating the new site to him and his commitment to God and country. Jerry was speechless when he saw the marker and permanent flagpole.

The church had supported Terry during Jerry's entire time away. Terry had worn many hats during her husband's absence. It had not been easy assuming the roles of mother and father, yard man and mechanic during those eight years. But life in the family had maintained some semblance of normalcy without Jerry because her family and friends from church had come to the rescue. They had always been eager to help in any way they could. She couldn't recall a Sunday at church when someone didn't say, "Have you heard anything?" So it was quite a celebration when Jerry returned.

At the church reception during the receiving line, the freed captive reconnected with many of the same high school students he had admonished to pray for him on that last Sunday back in 1965. As they came up to him with hugs and handshakes, he hardly recognized them. They were now adults themselves— they had careers, many of them were married, and several had children of their own. He thought to himself that these were some of the ones God had used as instruments for praying for his well-being while he had been in prison. It was a weekend filled with great rejoicing.

The following Monday, however, he awakened with only one thought.

He told his children as they left for classes that day, "Come home, Tommy, as soon as you're out from school—you, too, Lori. There's something I want us to do together." That afternoon, Jerry took both of them to a local Honda motorbike dealership and purchased a 100cc bike for Tommy and a 70cc bike for Lori.

"I can't believe it!" Tommy said, examining his shiny new motorbike. "I kept asking Mom if I could get one while you were gone, but Mom kept saying wait until you got back! When can we go riding?"

Lori simply stood beside hers, wide eyed with amazement. "Daddy, is this mine?"

"Yes, it is," Jerry answered her, "and I think you will like riding it. I'll show you how."

As the weeks progressed, Jerry found the phone ringing constantly with requests for speaking engagements and interviews. The first month home, his calendar quickly filled with an event every day.

Looking over his schedule one morning, however, he saw penciled into the only empty day that week "Ride motorbikes with Tommy." It was written in his son's handwriting, a gentle reminder he might need to slow down.

But nothing compared to the momentous day around the first of May when he and Terry received an elegant invitation in the mail: their presence was requested, along with all returning prisoners of war from Vietnam, at a seated dinner at the White House.

CHAPTER 19

A WALK IN LAFAYETTE PARK

MAY 24–25, 1973

EIGHTY-FIVE-YEAR-OLD IRVING BERLIN had just finished leading the thirteen hundred dinner guests on the White House lawn in singing his famous anthem "God Bless America." Emotions soared under the sprawling dinner tent. Jerry continued to be exuberant with happiness and thoughts of freedom.

At the finish of formal entertainment for the evening, most guests acted on President Nixon's invitation to tour the White House—as they pleased and unaccompanied. The Curtises followed others upstairs to admire guest apartments, especially the Lincoln Bedroom, with its massive rosewood bed. It was thrilling to be able to roam freely through the historic rooms.

When they came back downstairs, it was obvious from the sounds of merriment and dancing that the revelry was going to continue—and in fact it did, until past 2:00 a.m. Jerry looked at his watch: nearly midnight.

"Let's head back to our hotel," he said. Terry nodded in agreement.

He stopped to ask an attendant the easiest way out and was shown to the White House door facing Lafayette Park. Exiting here, they turned right, walked down through the guard gate, and were about to get a taxi when Jerry asked his wife if she would like to walk back. Their hotel, the Statler, was only a couple of blocks away.

"Okay," Terry said, and they made their way along brick sidewalks through Lafayette Park. The rain had stopped, but the deluge of the past thirty-six hours had left the air clean-smelling, fresh, and surprisingly not too muggy even for a May evening in the capital. Streets were still wet, and at this hour there was little traffic. The sound of Les Brown's band continued faintly in the distance from the other side of the White House. It had been a perfect evening.

As they strolled along, Jerry thought about the past three months. They had been a mind-numbing whirlwind of activities: parades, speaking engagements, television appearances. It seemed everyone in the United States wanted to hear from the returning POWs.

Many of the men who had experienced life under the atheistic Communist regime for so long wanted to get their stories out—wanted their fellow countrymen to know what had happened to them. Jerry had made a pledge to God that for as long as he lived, whenever he was asked to share, he would. He remained certain God had been with him and was the only reason any of them had made it home.

Returning to freedom caused no problems for him personally. As he would often say when he spoke to groups, "Freedom is easy to live with—it's when freedom is taken away that living becomes hard."

However, he and Terry already were discovering what some of the challenges were going to be moving forward. Disagreements mostly concerned the children. Jerry wished to be their father now more than ever, but he believed in strict discipline. Terry, who had had complete control for so long, found it extremely difficult to share her role in decisions pertaining to Tommy and Lori's behavior. It would prove to be a lifelong challenge for them.

As the couple walked along, Jerry placed his hand on his wife's shoulder. Such a small thing, but a tender pleasure he had missed. At least his mind seemed to be settling down, like something that unwinds slowly but has not quite completed the process. He hadn't really thought through all that had happened to him while in prison. He guessed that would come—he had no idea in what a dramatic way.

They arrived back at the Statler, along with several other couples, who evidently had decided to take advantage of a lovely evening for walking also. They were all exhausted. Jerry went to sleep that night as soon as his head hit the pillow.

In the early morning hours, however, a dream startled the newly repatriated prisoner awake—a dream so vivid, it caused him to react violently in his sleep. The same scenario would reccur often for several years to come. He dreamed he was climbing over a wall to freedom, as hard and as fast as he could. But beneath him, Communist guards grabbed at his legs to pull him back down. He jabbed forcibly at them with his feet in an effort to get away and over that wall.

With his vigorous kicking, he had awakened Terry. He slid quietly out of bed and assured her everything was all right. His lovely wife, exhausted from the day's activities, rolled over, welcoming sleep again.

Jerry walked over to a chair next to the window and sat down. On the small side table, he noticed his Meerschaum pipe, another small pleasure he had missed in prison. He reached over, filled its bowl, and in the darkness, lit it. Pulling back the curtains slightly, he looked out over the streets of Washington, DC, and took a deep breath. From where he sat, he could catch a glimpse of the White House, and beyond it, the Washington Monument in the distance.

So many things were different from when he had left the country in 1965. Pizza could be ordered to his doorstep—and during something called the Super Bowl. Men wore pants with flared ankle cuts, and women wore their hair piled sky-high on top of their heads. Neil Armstrong had walked on the moon, and Boeing had introduced the first 747 jumbo jet.

And enormously consequential national events had happened during the time he was imprisoned in Vietnam. Dr. Martin Luther King Jr. had been assassinated, followed two months later by Senator Robert Kennedy.

When he had returned to Louisiana, the state was still a hotbed of adjustment for integration. He himself, as a member of the military, was accustomed to being around people from various ethnic backgrounds. But the country continued to struggle.

Those were not the only social changes evident in society, however. He and Terry had gone to a movie together just a few weeks prior. The film, *Pete 'n' Tillie*, dealt with adult themes totally unlike anything Jerry had been accustomed to seeing in movies before he left the States. And when Walter Matthau grabbed Carol Burnett's derriere on the big screen, Jerry walked out of the movie theater. Things had changed.

It was well past midnight, and the deep quiet produced by plush carpet and thick curtains engulfed his hotel room. Suddenly, Jerry's mind seemed completely still, truly at peace for the first time since his release. He knew his body was getting stronger every day. The circles under his eyes were fading, and he was gaining a little weight. And right now, he seemed to be able to think with an exquisite clarity.

He ruminated over the days and weeks and years of his ordeal as a prisoner of war in North Vietnam. He thought first about his shoot-down—the rush to get away from the crash site, the hiding, the capture. He shook his head in the darkness and thought once more how he wished he had been able to rescue Will Forby that day back in 1965.

The event of the shoot-down of this one rescue Huskie would turn out to have specific historic military significance. His crew chief, Bill Robinson, and his pararescue jumper, Neil Black, became the longest-held enlisted prisoners of war in the history of the United States. While in prison, senior officers had led these two men in officer training, and later Air Force officials honored that, giving both men wartime commissions as officers when they were repatriated.

Jerry was proud of both men and their accomplishments. His thoughts now drifted to his copilot, Duane Martin. He had learned the young man had lived in the jungle for a few days before being caught by the Pathet Lao. While in captivity, Duane had met another downed pilot, Dieter Dengler.

Together, the two men attempted a daring escape before Duane was tragically killed.

In addition, out of six-hundred-plus POWs in Hanoi, twenty-five were awarded the Air Force Cross. Four of those would come from that rescue event alone: Jerry and his entire helicopter crew.

God, be with Duane's family. Comfort them and his children . . .

He sat still a moment. The area of Hoa Lo Prison dubbed Heartbreak Hotel was where his ordeal in Hanoi, North Vietnam, had begun. He remembered those initial days of confusion and bewilderment.

Jerry recalled his first Christmas Eve in prison. It was that night he had sensed God's presence so vividly. He had wrestled to come to grips with the nightmarish reality of his situation, and he had railed at God until he recognized the wrongness of that attitude.

He remembered the complete peace produced from his submission to God's authority surrounding him during that night of deep darkness, and it had followed him throughout his imprisonment. It was with him even now in the quiet of his hotel room.

It is a good thing we can't see into the future. Had I known during those first few days of capture just how long I would be there, I don't know what I would have done.

He chuckled to himself in the darkness at the remembrance of his first shower, when he had looked up to see, scrawled on the wall, "Smile, You're on Candid Camera." Over the years in prison, many other POWs had seen that message, sometimes in different places in the bathing area, and everyone had asked around about it.

We never did find out who wrote that on the shower wall!

He thought how he and all the other POWs had fought so hard to stay connected with one another. He remembered when he first learned the tap code—how he had practiced on a banana peel and had wondered if he would ever be proficient with it. He smiled: by the end of seven and a half years, he had been able to learn two foreign languages using the tap code while in solitary, then became proficient in those languages in the larger cell groups.

Now, for the first time in a long while, he thought back to the torture he had endured on several occasions, the excruciating pain from physical torture and the excruciating pain from solitary confinement—both conditions capable of taking a man to the brink of his mental faculties.

It had been proved over and over that men could indeed come to the end of what they could bear, physically and mentally, even men who were strong in their faith, their courage, and their commitment. They had learned that every man has a breaking point.

Seeing all of them earlier at dinner, dressed in formal military attire, polished and shining, had been an incredible sight. He had seen the man he led in a simple Communion service tapped through their adjoining cell walls; he saw most of his former cellmates, including the young man who had passed an empty plate during worship services in prison. They had all been there at the White House dinner. And he heard about many others with whom he had not shared a cell but knew only by name, like Mike Christian, who was known for his remarkable commitment to a scrap of fabric.

Unlike the evening they had just experienced, in prison the POWs had lived day in and day out without any tangible

symbols representing their nation or military status—no uniforms, no insignias, no patches, no emblems, and no American
flags. As months had turned into years, they often had looked
for ways to demonstrate their allegiance to their country. These
token tributes always had to be performed quietly and discreetly, to keep guards from seeing or hearing their pledges
or patriotic songs—behavior strictly forbidden and punished
if caught.

During one of his infrequent showers at Camp Unity, Mike
had spotted a dirty rag floating in the open sewer gutter and
suddenly had an idea. He sneaked the cloth back to his cell
and formulated a plan. He would need to make a needle out of
bamboo; he would need a scrap of blue material from someone's
prison uniform, red tile dust, and a little water. And he would
need to pull threads out of his thin blanket to use for sewing.

Deep into the night, while his cellmates slept, Mike would
sit in the corner under the dim lightbulb hanging from the
ceiling. He sewed the blue patch in one corner of the dingy
cloth he had whitened as best he could with bits of soap. Next,
he formed a red paste with the tile dust and water to make red
stripes. Then he sewed a few stars onto the blue patch using his
bamboo needle and blanket thread.

It had been crudely fashioned, ragged around the edges, and
with squiggly stripes. But when Mike had waved it at the end
of the cell one morning and said, "Hey, fellows, look at this!"
no one had any trouble recognizing what he had made. They all
had stood and quietly recited the Pledge of Allegiance.

Sitting in his hotel room, Jerry remembered the rest of the
story. Not long after Mike had finished his flag, guards came
into his cell and ordered everyone to strip down and go outside.

While ransacking the cell for contraband, they found Mike's flag. The guards waited to come back for him until that night—the nighttime interrogations were always the worst. And though there had not been any torture in the camp for several months, the prisoners could hear the beating begin as soon as the guards left with Mike for the torture room.

After several hours, the guards had pushed Mike back into the cell, or as one POW would say later, "At least what was left of him." His face was cut and bloodied all over, his arms hung limp, and he could barely walk. His cellmates comforted him as best they could.

Yet during the middle of the next night, when most were sleeping, several heard a scratching in the corner. They looked up, and there sat Mike, back under the dim lightbulb. His eyes were nearly swollen shut and his hands were trembling, but he had begun pulling threads out once more from his thin cotton blanket.

Jerry marveled again at the story of Mike's flags, of his dedication and commitment, just as he did the first time he had heard it in prison. The story had inspired all the POWs as they longed for the day when their symbols of freedom could be appreciated in the open once more.

Jerry prayed. *God, thank you for freedom, for this country. We may not always get everything right, but we live free. Thank you for that, and for bringing us home. Please honor the sacrifice of those who didn't make it back.*

But every one of them had experienced days when they weren't sure they could make it. For Jerry, sometimes it wasn't the years that had been so long. Sometimes it was enduring just the next five minutes. Jerry thought about his cellmate Will

Forby, who, when asked how in the world he had endured those years, had said, "One day at a time."

Jerry glanced down at his Bible lying on the table in front of the window. His thoughts drifted to the apostle Paul in the New Testament. Paul had endured prison many times, had experienced often the Roman versions of torture.

I've got a much greater appreciation now of the things Paul wrote, Jerry thought, *because I know firsthand something of the pain and torture the apostle often sustained.* He recalled Paul's words to a struggling church:

I am persuaded, that neither death, nor life, nor angels, nor principalities, nor powers, nor things present, nor things to come, nor height, nor depth, nor any other creature, shall be able to separate us from the love of God, which is in Christ Jesus our Lord.

Jerry now knew the truth of this. He prayed, *So many times, God, your presence was felt just at a moment of great need. Not anything I ever endured, God—not the torture, not the pain, not the loneliness, not the fear—was able to separate me from your love.*

He continued looking out the window of their hotel room. It had begun to drizzle, and raindrops clustered on the glass like crystals. Across the room, he could hear the gentle, rhythmic breathing of his wife as she slept.

All through the years, Jerry had known Terry would remain faithful and continue raising their children. Eight years to be apart from family is a long time. Jerry admitted to himself that even though they had been through deep waters, there might be deep waters ahead. But he knew God would be with them.

Jerry glanced back out over the streets of Washington. The rain had stopped, and the first few scattered rays of dawn could be seen breaking in the eastern sky. He knew the POW experience would forever define his life. But Jerry prayed, *Looking back, God, I can see the trace of your hand all through those years. You never left me. You always gave me just enough light to continue on.*

TEN YEARS LATER

THOMAS "JERRY" CURTIS HAD BEEN at Academy High School in Little River-Academy, Texas, for several years, but he didn't require his students to address him by his retirement rank of colonel. He instructed his students to use "señor," since as head of the language department, he taught mainly Spanish. They all knew he had learned to speak it while in prison in North Vietnam.

When he had applied for the teaching position, the superintendent couldn't believe how Jerry had learned foreign languages. Jerry had explained that POWs wrote Spanish and French words on bits and pieces of toilet paper and then hid them in their toilet buckets so guards couldn't discover them. During the latter years of his captivity, he had been instructed by several men who were fluent in both.

"Tell you what," the superintendent had said, "how about starting a foreign language department here at Academy High? We don't have one—we need that—and until you get enough classes in foreign languages going, you can fill in with world geography." And thus began an incredibly rewarding second career for the retired wartime hero.

Over the years, Jerry had discovered he loved to teach and relished interaction with the students. Above all else, his primary goal was motivating them to learn.

On this day, with the Thanksgiving holiday just around the corner, several stayed after class to ask him about his wartime experiences. So he sat down with them and began to tell his story.

"I was shot down trying to rescue a fighter pilot whose F-105 had taken a hit. Later, he and I became cellmates. Now he is in education too—principal of a Christian school," said Jerry.

His students listened intently. They asked for more stories about his years in prison in North Vietnam and seemed interested mostly in three things: what he ate, did he ever kill anybody, and had he been tortured. Jerry answered all their questions.

And he used his experience to teach them about their own opportunities. "I didn't choose to be captured or to be a prisoner for nearly eight years. But never think you cannot do something. You can accomplish more than you think you can. Throughout life, you are going to have setbacks." The students hadn't moved a muscle, so Jerry went on.

"If you have a dream, it's never too late to pursue it. Look at me—I had always wanted to finish college and teach, and now I'm doing that. And for me, faith and family have always been the most important things. I've had a relationship with

God since I was twelve years old. Granted, my faith has grown since then—in fact, it grew a lot while I was in prison, as you can imagine. Actually, it grew for most of the men there. Two of my friends in prison even composed a verse to a song we sing in church sometimes. Do you know the hymn 'How Great Thou Art'?"

Several nodded yes.

"Well, listen to a verse they made up. We sang it together while we were in Hanoi:

In foreign lands, you're even there to guide me,
Your Holy Spirit in my heart yet dwells;
When nights are cold, I feel your light inside me,
Imparting warmth to these cold hostile cells.

"God was with me every day, during the worst times— maybe *especially* through the worst times. And he is with me now. He will not always do things the way you want him to, but he will be with you wherever you allow him to be," Jerry said.

The teacher stood up, and the students thanked him for staying and talking with them. On this particular fall day at Academy High School, just before Thanksgiving, they left his classroom and planned how to spend the vacation days stretching ahead of them.

Jerry picked up the exam papers, placing them into his brief-case, a weekend's worth of work ahead, but not for Thanksgiving Day. That day would be spent feasting on the huge dinner Terry was planning for all of them—for Jerry and Terry, for Tom and his family, and for Lori and hers.

As Jerry walked down the deserted corridors of the high

school, he passed door after door, classrooms shut and locked for the holidays. The janitors were already sweeping and cleaning the floors.

When he reached the exit leading to the teachers' parking lot, he stopped and looked down at the door's metal push bar. One of his POW buddies had recently sent out a letter to the POW community, something most of them did frequently to keep in touch with one another. A sentiment from that message suddenly came to Jerry's mind.

"My former cellmate is right," he chuckled to himself. "No matter what else might be happening, any day is a good day so long as there's a handle on your side of the door." He pushed it open and stepped out into the warm sunshine of a Texas fall afternoon.

ACKNOWLEDGMENTS

THIS BOOK ACTUALLY BEGAN many years ago—or at least my interest in the Vietnam War was kindled years ago. As a young college student sitting in classes at the University of California–Davis during the late sixties and early seventies, I watched as friends protested the war through hunger strikes on campus and as my military family members flew into harm's way every day. Controversy laced all of it.

In hindsight, two things become clear. The first is that brave men did what they were asked to do, and many died in the process.

The second is more reflective. It comes as we contemplate the events of those turbulent years: we as a nation did not properly recognize the unbelievably difficult circumstances surrounding the return of all our veterans, officer or enlisted, ground troop or airmen.

Against this backdrop comes the story of our POWs, a story comprising one of the most heroic sagas in the annals of American military history. Under horrific conditions and constant physical and mental pressures, these six-hundred-plus men (an even larger number if we count those held in Laos and in South Vietnam) found a way not just to survive but to return with honor.

The subject of this book, COL Thomas "Jerry" Curtis, would want us to remember all those who returned without a hero's welcome, to honor them and their sacrifice, and to remember all our veterans who have served and are serving today this great land of freedom we live in.

So first and foremost, I acknowledge and graciously thank all those who have served our country and who are serving even now.

Next, I am so fortunate to have had one of the premier people working in publishing—Greg Johnson, president of Wordserve Literary and FaithHappenings.com—read my proposal and get it into the right hands. This project would still be a dream rather than reality if not for your expertise.

Then, of course, to the "right hands," Tyndale House Publishers: thank you so much for appreciating the story of COL Thomas "Jerry" Curtis and wanting others to read and be inspired by it also. Specific thanks to Carol Traver for recognizing the potential of this story and to Jonathan Schindler for sharpening the nuances while maintaining its integrity. You both set a very high bar for what "professional" means in the publishing world.

Yet no writer undertakes a major project such as this without many people coming alongside him or her to help and to contribute their gifts and talents.

First, to Dr. and Mrs. Melvin Holder, who read each chapter as I produced it, submitting thoughts, corrections, suggestions. You truly have been a godsend. But especially to Bren—your encouragement along the way meant so much. I appreciate your input, not just for the manuscript, but your prayer input as well, even in moments of last-minute urgency. (The hyphen is for you!)

Second, to a young woman who helped produce and design the original proposal and currently assists me with all things "computer," Jenn Korver—it is such a comfort to know I can count on you for your knowledge and willingness to help at any time. And to Jim Wortham, Jenn's dad, thanks for all the production aspects of photos, scans, videos, and other visuals necessary as we worked to gather material for the manuscript. I am always amazed at the quality of your work. In addition, Sarah Beth Sandel, professional photographer, helped with photos, and I'm so delighted God allowed our paths to cross. I know he has great plans in store for you.

Then, of course, thanks to the illustrator for this project, Bret Melvin. This is the second book Bret has illustrated for me and (hopefully!) will not be the last. Your drawings add that extra dimension to bring life to the entire story. God has given you an incredible talent. Thank you for using it here!

But I can honestly say this project would have been greatly hindered if not for my husband, who, when deadlines came around, stood in the gap as chief cook and bottle washer, without complaining and, in fact, joyfully. He is a Proverbs 31 man! Thank you so much for being who you are to me.

This last will sound cliché . . . and it would be if not for the simple fact that it's true: God led me to this project. How he did that is a story for another day, but suffice it to say, his hand was in it from the start. That has been reaffirmed time and time again over the past two years, sometimes in the most surprising ways imaginable.

I hardly know how to express my thanks to him for allowing me to be the one to tell the amazing story of COL Thomas "Jerry" Curtis. I pray it brings hope to you, the reader. It is honest—sometimes raw, sometimes joyful—just the way life really is. But it gives the most incredible look at something that should always bring us to a complete standstill: the trace of God's hand in our daily lives. After all, he is the master Storyteller.

ABOUT THE AUTHORS

CAROLE ENGLE AVRIETT is a former writer and editor for *Southern Living* magazine. In addition to leading women's conferences throughout the United States, Canada, and Brazil, where she and her husband serve as missionaries during the summer months, Carole has authored two Bible studies. She currently resides in Florida.

COL THOMAS "JERRY" CURTIS (USAF, RET) is an Air Force Cross recipient, a Daughters of the American Revolution Medal of Honor recipient, and a sought-after speaker by schools, church groups, VFW chapters, Rotary Clubs, and other veteran groups and patriotic organizations. Jerry currently resides in Texas.

Capt. Thomas "Jerry" Curtis at Nakhon Phanom Royal Thai Air Force Base (NKP), Thailand, summer 1965, one month before shoot-down and capture. HH-43 in background. (Curtis collection)

Thomas "Jerry" Curtis (left) on release day, Feb. 12, 1973, walking to board C-141 at Gia Lam Airport, Hanoi, Vietnam, with USAF escort officer (middle) and Will Forby (right), the downed fighter pilot Curtis was attempting to rescue when he himself was shot down. (Curtis collection)

Dinner celebration in honor of Son Tay Raid Special Ops Forces given by H. Ross Perot in 1973. Curtis (left), Clint Eastwood (center), member of Special Ops Forces (right). (Curtis collection)

Curtis inspecting the "jungle penetrator," the hoist seat extended from the helicopter into the jungle to pick up airmen. (Curtis collection)

Tin-roofed hooches erected as a radar and rescue post at NKP, 1965. (USAF Air Rescue Operations: National Archives)

Refueling an HH-43 at NKP. (USAF Air Rescue Operations: National Archives)

Curtis (right) with Maj. Robert W. Wilson (left) just after rescue when his F-105 was shot down in Nugia Pass, Laos, June 1965. After ejection, Wilson landed in a tree, and Curtis's crew lowered the jungle penetrator from HH-43 to pull the pilot out. (Curtis collection)

Curtis (back to camera) checking an HH-43 just before a rescue mission. Pararescue jumper Neil Black (left) was part of Curtis's crew when his helicopter was shot down on Sept. 20, 1973, and was also captured by the North Vietnamese. (Curtis collection)

Curtis (back to camera) adjusting survival vest before flying a rescue mission. (Curtis collection)

Curtis examining map of Laos
and North Vietnam for a mission.
(USAF Air Rescue Operations:
National Archives)

Terry Curtis sharing Jerry's first letter from prison in 1970, five years after capture,
with son, Tommy, and daughter, Lori. (Curtis collection)

Release day in Hanoi, Feb. 12, 1973, as prisoners get off buses at Gia Lam Airport to be repatriated by US military officials. Curtis in far back row. (Curtis collection)

Jubilation from released prisoners as the C-141 Starlifter leaves North Vietnam air space: flight to freedom during Operation Homecoming, Feb. 12, 1973. Curtis in second row, extreme right side, next to Will Forby, the man he was trying to rescue when captured.

Home at last: the Curtises
together again after eight years,
just behind couple in front,
also a returning POW. (UPI
photo, Sun Herald, Biloxi,
Mississippi)

Son, Tom, and daughter, Lori, (near airplane) running to greet their dad for the first
time after arriving home, Feb. 15, 1973. (Curtis collection)

White House dinner invitation,
May 24, 1973. (Curtis collection)

Col. and Mrs. Curtis with Gen. P. K. Carlton at awards ceremony where Curtis
received the Air Force Cross. (Curtis collection)

Two former POWs reunited: Col. Joe Kittinger, USAF (Ret.), internationally known balloonist who set free-fall record from 19 miles above the earth as featured on cover of *Life* magazine, 1960, and enshrined in Aviation Hall of Fame, and Col. Curtis at 2015 event in Orlando, where Col. Curtis was guest speaker. Kittinger was shot down over North Vietnam and taken prisoner on May 11, 1972. (Photo courtesy of Dr. Stan Hand)

The National Society of the Daughters of the American Revolution, Medal of Honor, awarded to Col. Thomas J. Curtis. (Curtis collection)

POW bracelet campaign represented one of the primary ways families promoted awareness of POWs/MIAs during the war. More 500 of these were returned to him after Curtis came home in 1973. Curtis answered each one with a personal letter of thanks. (Curtis collection)

LIST OF PRISON CAMPS AND APPROXIMATE DATES OF JERRY'S IMPRISONMENT

1. September 20, 1965—Shoot-down
2. September 28/30, 1965–end of October/November 1, 1965—"Heartbreak Hotel" (section of Hoa Lo Prison, dubbed "Hanoi Hilton," downtown Hanoi)
3. November 1, 1965–April 1966—"The Zoo" ("Pigsty," possibly an old French film studio turned into a prison in a southwest suburb of Hanoi)
4. April 1966–February 1967—"Briarpatch" (prison camp 35 miles northwest of Hanoi)
5. February 1967–June 1967—"Vegas" (section of "Hanoi Hilton")
6. June 1967–August 1967—"The Power Plant" (deserted area of a thermal power plant in northern Hanoi)
7. August 1967–October 1967—"The School" (another area of a thermal power plant used to contain POWs)
8. October 1967–December 1969—"Vegas" (section of "Hanoi Hilton")
9. December 1969–July 1970—"Camp Hope" (Son Tay prison camp, located 22 miles northwest of Hanoi)

10. July 1970–November 1970—"Camp Faith" (Dan Hoi prison camp, 9 miles northwest of Hanoi)
11. November 1970–May 1972—"Camp Unity" (section of "Hanoi Hilton")
12. May 1972–January 1973—"Dogpatch" (7 miles from the China border)
13. January 1973–February 12, 1973—"Camp Unity" (section of "Hanoi Hilton")

MAP OF APPROXIMATE LOCATIONS OF PRISON CAMPS

NOTES

CHAPTER 1: THE DINNER PARTY

4 *The role of master of ceremonies . . . pictures with as many as desired:* Original White House program for the event (private collection of memorabilia), Col. and Mrs. Thomas "Jerry" Curtis.

4 *Remembering the evening years later . . . a generally relaxed attitude:* Stephen Bauer, *At Ease in the White House: Social Life as Seen by a Presidential Military Aide* (Lanham, MD: Taylor Trade, 2004), 77.

4–5 *The menu was kept simple:* Original menu card (private collection of memorabilia), Col. and Mrs. Curtis.

5 *The returning POWs . . . brought them home:* "He [Nixon] was a hero to us. He will always be revered by us as a group because he got us home." Marine Capt. (Ret.) Orson Swindle, former Assist. Sec. of Commerce during the Reagan Administration (POW 1966–1973), Associated Press, "Nixon Library Hosts 40th Reunion for POWs," May 23, 2013, http://www.military.com/daily-news/2013/05/23/nixon-library-hosts-40th-reunion-for-vietnam-pows.html.

7–8 *Faith Baptist Church in Kaiserslautern:* Archives, Faith Baptist Church, Kaiserslautern, Germany.

10 *took his life just nine days after the dinner party:* ABC Nightly News Archives, *ABC's Wide World of Entertainment.*

CHAPTER 2: NAKHON PHANOM

13 *Nakhon Phanom Royal Thai Air Force Base . . . rescue and support missions:* Wayne Mutza, *Kaman H-43: An Illustrated History* (Atglen, PA: Schiffer, 1998), 64–82.

13 *inadequate personnel, nonexistent doctrine, and ill-suited aircraft:* Earl H. Tilford, *Setup: What the Air Force Did in Vietnam and Why* (Maxwell Air Force Base, AL: Air University Press, 1991).

14 *The HH-43 had a top speed . . . could push the helicopter's fuel capabilities to the limit:* Mutza, *Kaman H-43*, 64–82.

CHAPTER 3: THE SECRET WAR IN LAOS

21–22 *The CIA established the base . . . a natural ally for the United States:* Emily Rauhala, "Fond Farewells: Vang Pao, Guerrilla Leader, 81," *Time*, December 14, 2011, http://content.time.com/time/specials/packages /article/0,28804,2101745_2102136_2102247,00.html; Douglas Martin, "Gen. Vang Pao, Laotian Who Aided US, Dies at 81," *New York Times*, January 8, 2011, http://www.nytimes.com/2011/01/08/world /asia/08vangpao.html.

30 *Royal Lao regulars had been ambushed by Pathet Lao forces:* Kenneth Conboy, *The War in Laos (1960–1975)* (London: Osprey, 1989).

CHAPTER 4: THE SHOOT-DOWN

38 *They all thought . . . were following along behind them:* Martin's capture, and that of another downed pilot, Dieter Dengler, was the subject of a motion picture titled *Rescue Dawn*, director Werner Herzog, 2007. For a further account of Martin's story, see Stuart Rochester and Frederick Kiley, *Honor Bound* (Annapolis, MD: Naval Institute Press, 1998), 48–50, 280–82.

CHAPTER 5: HEARTBREAK HOTEL

45–46 *The world knew this dungeon-like structure as Maison Centrale . . . entered its gates:* William S. Logan, *Hanoi: Biography of a City* (Sydney: University of New South Wales Press, 2000), 67–68.

51 *a type of code used in previous POW situations:* Robinson Risner, *The Passing of the Night* (Old Saybrook, CT: Konecky & Konecky, 1973), 32.

52 *scratched into the cell wall this soul-saving grid:* Ibid.

52 *required to memorize and use the tap code:* Stuart Rochester and Frederick Kiley, *Honor Bound* (Annapolis, MD: Naval Institute Press, 1998), 101–106, 134.

52 *"It is not good for man to be alone."* See Genesis 2:18.

CHAPTER 6: CHAIN OF COMMAND

68 *old posters, film canisters, and damaged reels:* Stuart Rochester and Frederick Kiley, *Honor Bound* (Annapolis, MD: Naval Institute Press, 1998), 128–30.

CHAPTER 8: BRIARPATCH HUMOR

87 *Some POWs later described him . . . evoked alternately scorn and terror:* Stuart Rochester and Frederick Kiley, *Honor Bound* (Annapolis, MD: Naval Institute Press, 1998), 212.

88 *Many POWs began developing their own signature sneeze . . . "dismal as ever, but normal":* Ibid., 417.

93 *One of the POWs began to sing . . . "Do they do this often?":* Ibid., 194–98.

94 *One POW, Lee Ellis . . . "shackles of fear and worry":* Lee Ellis, *Leading with Honor: Leadership Lessons from the Hanoi Hilton* (Cumming, GA: FreedomStar Media, 2012), 74.

CHAPTER 9: BREAKING POINT

96 *Code of Conduct contains six tenets:* The Code of Conduct for Members of the United States Armed Forces:

  I. I am an American, fighting in the forces which guard my country and our way of life. I am prepared to give my life in their defense.

  II. I will never surrender of my own free will. If in command, I will never surrender the members of my command while they still have the means to resist.

  III. If I am captured I will continue to resist by all means available. I will make every effort to escape and aid others to escape. I will accept neither parole nor special favors from the enemy.

  IV. If I become a prisoner of war, I will keep faith with my fellow prisoners. I will give no information or take part in any action which might be harmful to my comrades. If I am senior, I will take command. If not, I will obey the lawful orders of those appointed over me and will back them up in every way.

  V. When questioned, should I become a prisoner of war, I am required to give name, rank, service number and date of birth. I will evade answering further questions to the utmost of my ability. I will make no oral or written statements disloyal to my country and its allies or harmful to their cause.

  VI. I will never forget that I am an American, fighting for freedom, responsible for my actions, and dedicated to the principles which made my country free. I will trust in my God and in the United States of America.

98 *Risner himself, one of the staunchest of men . . . but within reason:* Robinson Risner, *The Passing of the Night* (Old Saybrook, CT: Konecky & Konecky, 1973), 31.

99 *With his heart pounding and hands sweating . . . "paid for it with blood":* Admiral Jeremiah A. Denton, *When Hell Was in Session* (Los Angeles: World Net Daily, 1975), 95.

99 *Admiral Denton would call the month of July 1966 perhaps the most torture-filled month of North Vietnam POW history:* Ibid., 93.

100 *"In terms of prolonged misery, no prisoners suffered more than the men confined at Briarpatch":* Stuart Rochester and Frederick Kiley, *Honor Bound* (Annapolis, MD: Naval Institute Press, 1998), 159.

CHAPTER 11: THE MIDDLE YEARS

125 *"Almost all of the captives . . . crisis of the spirit at some juncture":* Stuart Rochester and Frederick Kiley, *Honor Bound* (Annapolis, MD: Naval Institute Press, 1998), 445.

125–126 *"the melting experience":* Ibid.

127 *the Power Plant . . . and other smaller facilities:* Ibid., 319–23.

CHAPTER 12: TIES THAT BIND

139 *an officer . . . whose "patience cannot be lost":* Claude D. Clower, CDR, USN, Official Military Evaluation of Thomas Curtis, 5 Nov. 1973.

140 *One POW noted . . . "sounded like a cabinet factory":* Stuart Rochester and Frederick Kiley, *Honor Bound* (Annapolis, MD: Naval Institute Press, 1998), 294.

141 *Howard "Howie" E. Rutledge . . . "we learned to communicate with anything and everything":* Howard and Phyllis Rutledge with Mel and Lyla White, *In the Presence of Mine Enemies* (Old Tappan, NJ: Revell, 1973), 49.

CHAPTER 13: A WAR OF WORDS

161 *And Jerry began the tedious task . . . opportunity to implement it:* Later, after their release, then–Rear Admiral Stockdale had this to say about the young man who needed coaching during his first attempt at remembering BACK-US while washing dishes at an outdoor sink in Vegas: "This officer performed the duties of a highly classified nature in an extremely diligent and competent manner. The assignment, which was available only to volunteers who exhibited the highest level of intelligence and personal integrity and unswerving loyalty to country, was willingly performed at significant risk in an enemy controlled prison environment. His productive sustained performance of this demanding task required long hours of mental concentration and training over a prolonged period of time while under constant surveillance and harassment by the enemy." James Stockdale, REAR ADM, USN, Official Military Evaluation of Thomas Curtis, 27 July 1973.

Another official evaluation said, "His high personal standards and unusual courage were displayed in his communications effort . . . he boldly 'flagged' building to building daily to complete the communications chain to the SRO." Elmo Baker, LT COL, USAF, Official Military Evaluation of Thomas Curtis, 28 Sept. 1973.

Yet another senior officer later reported, "He was chosen for this job because of his excellent judgment, good ideas, leadership and dedication . . . his personal example helped keep the morale and resistance posture of the entire squadron at a high level. He spent hours communicating with POWs in other buildings in order to keep our command channel functioning and for morale and educational purposes even though it was a physically demanding job and subject to punishment if caught." Carlyle S. Harris, COL, USAF, Official Military Evaluation of Thomas Curtis, 9 Oct. 1973.

CHAPTER 14: COMMITTED

176–77   *Author John Gargus, in his book documenting the raid . . . "It just couldn't be happening!":* John Gargus, *The Son Tay Raid: American POWs in Vietnam Were Not Forgotten* (College Station, TX: Texas A & M University Press, 2007), 203.

177   *the courageous rescue attempt . . . had been frantically moved back into downtown Hanoi:* Years later, after his release, Jerry was able to meet many of the men who had participated in the daring rescue attempt and was able to thank them personally. In late 1973, H. Ross Perot flew all POWs and Special Ops personnel involved with the Son Tay Raid to California for an elaborate celebration in their honor.

An array of celebrities attended, including Clint Eastwood, who sat next to Jerry during dinner. It was a memorable evening. Jerry also learned the pilot who flew the HH-3 that landed in the compound that night was personal friend Major Herb Kalen, who was in flight school with him. Kalen's helicopter, call sign Banana, had been rigged with pyrotechnics in order to blow it up afterward since officials knew the chopper's blades would hit a tree in the middle of the compound during landing—one of many details learned from satellite photographs before the raid. Kalen and his crew plus all the other men involved had executed their mission perfectly.

"You may not have brought us home that night, but our spirits soared when we found out about it in prison," Jerry told the Special Ops men who had come to Son Tay to rescue the POWs imprisoned there—he himself one of them. "You restored our hope that we hadn't been forgotten by our country—nothing in Hoa Lo prison was the same after that. It gave all of us a real reason to stay committed."

CHAPTER 15: THE HANOI HILTON "UNIVERSITY"

182–83   *Among the languages offered . . . "the appetite for knowledge was great":* Stuart Rochester and Frederick Kiley, *Honor Bound* (Annapolis, MD: Naval Institute Press, 1998), 545–46.

191–92   *they decided on a few favorites . . . chapter 13 of 1 Corinthians:* James E. Ray, "The Secret of Our Survival," *The Guideposts Treasury of Hope* (New York: Random House, 1996), 295–99.

CHAPTER 16: THE 4TH ALLIED POW WING

208 *In his book . . . "the most decisive moment of the war.":* Admiral Jeremiah A. Denton, *When Hell Was in Session* (Los Angeles: World Net Daily, 1975), 236.

212 *One POW recalled, "The thud of eight hundred rubber-tire sandals coming together smartly was awesome.":* Stuart Rochester and Frederick Kiley, *Honor Bound* (Annapolis, MD: Naval Institute Press, 1998), 572.

CHAPTER 19: A WALK IN LAFAYETTE PARK

259–60 *While in captivity, Duane had met another downed pilot, Dieter Dengler. Together, the two men attempted a daring escape before Duane was tragically killed:* A movie was made of their story: *Rescue Dawn*, director Werner Herzog, 2007.

264 *"I am persuaded, that neither death, nor life . . . shall be able to separate us from the love of God, which is in Christ Jesus our Lord":* Romans 8:38-39.

EPILOGUE: TEN YEARS LATER

269 *Well, listen to a verse they made up . . . "to these cold hostile cells":* Written by Colonel Elmo Baker, USAF (Ret.) and Lieutenant Colonel Gene Smith, USAF (Ret.), in Hoa Lo Prison, Hanoi, North Vietnam.

Love memoirs?
Find your next great read at MemoirAddict.com!

At Memoir Addict, we find ordinary people with extraordinary stories.

Explore:

- updates on new releases
- additional stories from your favorite authors
- FREE first-chapter downloads
- discussion guides
- author videos and book trailers

- inspirational quotes to share on Pinterest, Twitter, and Facebook
- book reviews
- and so much more!

While you're there, check out our blog, featuring unique perspectives on memoirs from all facets of the publishing industry. From authors to acquisition directors to editors, we share our passion for storytelling. You'll get an insider's look at the craft of shaping a story into a captivating memoir.

Are you a memoir addict? Follow us on Twitter @MemoirAddict and on Facebook for updates on your favorite authors, free e-book promotions, contests, and more!

Plus, visit BookClubHub.net to

- download free discussion guides
- get book club recommendations
- sign up for Tyndale's book club and e-newsletters

MemoirAddict.com: ordinary people, extraordinary stories!

CP1001

Online Discussion
guide

TAKE *your* TYNDALE READING
EXPERIENCE *to the* NEXT LEVEL

A FREE discussion guide for this book
is available at bookclubhub.net, perfect
for sparking conversations in your book
group or for digging deeper into the text
on your own.

www.bookclubhub.net

*You'll also find free discussion guides for
other Tyndale books, e-newsletters, e-mail
devotionals, virtual book tours, and more!*

CP0071